Gordon's
Great Escape
Southeast Asia

Gordon's
Great Escape
Southeast Asia

Photographer Emma Lee Text Gordon Ramsay and Lauren Abery
Art Director Patrick Budge Food Stylists Lauren Abery and Lisa Harrison
Home Economist Lisa Harrison Props Stylist Emma Thomas

HarperCollins*Publishers*

Cook's notes

Spoon measures are level, unless otherwise specified:
1 tsp is equivalent to 5ml; 1 tbsp is equivalent to 15ml.

Use good-quality sea salt, freshly ground black pepper and fresh herbs for the best flavour.

Use large eggs unless otherwise suggested, ideally organic or free-range. If you are pregnant or in a vulnerable health group, avoid dishes using raw egg whites or lightly cooked eggs.

Individual ovens may vary in actual temperature by 10°C from the setting, so it is important to know your oven. Use an oven thermometer to check its accuracy.

Timings are provided as guidelines, with a description of colour or texture where appropriate, but readers should rely on their own judgement as to when a dish is properly cooked.

10 9 8 7 6 5 4 3 2 1

HarperCollins*Publishers*
77–85 Fulham Palace Road,
Hammersmith, London W6 8JB
www.harpercollins.co.uk

First published by HarperCollins*Publishers* 2011

Text © 2011 Gordon Ramsay
Photography © 2011 Emma Lee
Great Escape format and programme © 2011
One Potato Two Potato Ltd

Gordon Ramsay asserts the moral right to be identified as the author of this work.

A CIP catalogue record of this book is available from the British Library

ISBN 978-0-00-726704-0

Printed and bound in Great Britain by Butler, Tanner & Dennis Ltd, Frome, Somerset

Contents

Introduction

About 20 years ago, in my early days as a commis chef, I remember someone handing me this weird-looking stalk, which I soon learned was lemongrass. I was excited to discover an unfamiliar ingredient – what did it taste like, where did it come from, were there more like this? That day taught me that as a chef you never stop learning, a lesson that holds true today. While I felt confident cooking French cuisine, I was yet to discover the ingredients, flavours and cooking techniques of places further afield. On my first Great Escape to India, I found that the best way to understand the food of another nation is to experience it in the country itself. For my second Great Escape my taste buds were in for an unforgettable rollercoaster ride as I set off on a pilgrimage to experience the culinary delights of not one country but four: Thailand, Cambodia, Vietnam and Malaysia.

Thailand

Of the four countries on my itinerary, Thailand was the nation and cuisine I was most familiar with because I had visited it on a family holiday. I knew that at the forefront of Thai food is the creation of balance of sweet, sour, spicy, bitter and hot flavours, and that it has more to offer than the Thai green curries and Pad Thais that the West have adopted. It has long been said that some of the best food in Thailand can be found on the streets – and I have to agree. There is no shortage of street sellers, whose wares vary from barbecued chicken (*Gai yang*, page 208), green papaya salad (*Som tam*, page 71), deep-fried shrimp (Coconut prawns, page 43), to drinks. A successful street stall can, indeed, be more popular than a restaurant.

As in any country, Thai dishes vary from region to region. In Southern Thailand the food is spicy (they love cooking with chillies and some dishes will blow you away), but in this region you will also find lots of salads (like the *Kao Yum*) and, due to its close proximity to the sea, fish plays a major part in the diet. On my travels I ventured into a small village about one hour south of Ao Nang, where I spent the afternoon oyster fishing and was then taught some local dishes by a villager and expert called Ya. She spent hours creating the different curry pastes, but after all that effort I was relieved to see that each dish then took only moments to prepare – such as the *Khanom jeen* (page 168) and Prawn and stink bean stir-fry (page 122).

My journey then took me from the south to the north, as I travelled to Chiang Mai, one of the largest and most cultural cities in Thailand. It was there that I discovered the culture of Buddhist monks; in Thailand, Buddhism is the majority religion and you will often see monks going about their daily duties in their bright orange robes. Every day at around 6am the monks take to the streets, barefooted and carrying urns in which they collect food offerings from locals. Entering orders means you have to erase any ego and give up your worldly possessions, including money, so you rely on handouts to survive. One morning I removed my shoes and walked the pavements with the monks as their assistant; we were given mangoes, sticky rice, dried goods, meat, nuts and so much more. I am the first to admit that I am not a religious person, but I did find the generosity of the community astounding.

It is inevitable that with Buddhism playing such a large role in the lives of the Thai people, food has become interwoven with the religion. One of my favourite dishes that I discovered in Thailand was one I helped cook for a Buddhist house blessing; it was the *Gaeng hung lay* curry (page 170) which is traditionally served to monks at such ceremonies.

Cambodia

Often just viewed as the country in between Thailand and Vietnam, for me Cambodia is the forgotten kingdom. As a country that has gone through so much hardship – suffering genocide during the reign of the Khmer Rouge, occupation by the Vietnamese and subjected to military coups – Cambodia is finally on a slow path to recovery.

There is a charm about Cambodia; it feels to me how perhaps Thailand would have been over 15 years ago, before the arrival of mass tourism and consumerism. Arriving by plane, flying over field after field, the vastness of this country quickly became apparent. It is estimated that around 2 million people died during the genocide of the Khmer Rouge, while many others are thought to have died from starvation, and so many of the brave people I met on my travels round this country had stories to tell of those painful years. As the Khmer Rouge attempted to rewrite Cambodian history – to begin it again from the start of their rule – they destroyed all the literature and documentation they could find, including traditional family recipes and most food publications and cookbooks. As a result the country has had to develop a cuisine and a culture all over again since the collapse of the regime. I found it strange to be in a country that, in the twenty-first century, is still trying to establish its cuisine.

The biggest difference in Cambodian attitudes to food compared to the other countries I visited during this Great Escape, is that for many food is just sustenance. The ingredients used in Cambodian cooking are similar to those of Thailand and Vietnam, but the food is less spicy and more rustic. Cambodians have learnt how to make use of sources of flavour and protein that other countries avoid – from insects to unusual herbs, flowers and fruits. As a chef I have sampled many different foods, but in Cambodia I chewed my way through tarantulas, duck-egg foetus, crocodile, frogs and various insects. Travelling between the cities and villages, there is a big divide between the peasant food of the countryside, which lacks fresh spices and meat, to the upmarket city food that uses an array of ingredients, including imported goods.

My Cambodian journey began in the northern city of Siem Reap, famous for the Angkor Wat, built in the twelfth century but still the world's largest religious building. It was here that I learnt to cook traditional Cambodian dishes such as Fish amok (page 176). In the southern city of Phnom Penh I met an inspirational Cambodian chef called Luu Meng; he is paving the way for Cambodian cuisine as part of a new generation of innovative, creative chefs who are making it their mission to rediscover ancient Khmer cuisine. To find new inspiration, Luu regularly takes trips to the villages to seek out traditional recipes and also to see how people are cooking now. Taking my cue from Luu Meng, I travelled off to the jungle to be a guest at a tribal wedding, and this was the inspiration for the Khmer wild honey-glazed roast chicken (page 232) and Chocolate-covered toasted rice sticky squares (page 247).

I haven't even touched on my time in the charitable street kids organisation in Phnom Penh, cooking for Cambodian royalty or visiting a floating village; it is impossible to relate everything that happened on that action-packed trip! I left Cambodia with a real sense of the place; the people were friendly and warm and the experience left me excited to see how their cuisine and their country evolves over the coming years.

Malaysia

While the cuisine in Cambodia is still on a journey of discovery, that of Malaysia has been evolving for hundreds of years, and it was because of this, and because the country is a large, multi-cultural hub with many different communities and religions living alongside one another, that Malay food seemed the most diverse on this journey.

In this book there are many references to Nonya cuisine in dishes such as 'Nonya fried rice' or 'Nonya fried chicken'. Nonya cuisine is over 500 years old and has its roots in the time when the first Chinese settlers came to Malaysia. As they integrated with the community and married the Malays, so the two cuisines blended and new dishes were created using the influence of both. However, in addition to this Nonya cuisine the food in Malaysia also takes influence from countries such as India, Sri Lanka, China, Thailand and Indonesia.

The island of Penang is regarded as a food Mecca and the culinary capital of Malaysia. There you will find a plethora of street stalls selling Chicken satay (page 56) and *Nasi lemak* (page 214). Penang is just one big showcase of the food the country has to offer; the ingredients there are fairly Indian-inspired and feature a wide range of spices.

Vietnam

Like its neighbour Cambodia, Vietnam has suffered years of unrest – even before the 20-year Vietnam War. However, as a country it has made great speed in its recovery and over the past 15 years it has begun to show great economic growth.

In terms of their cuisine, the Vietnamese know what they like and stick to it, unlike the Malaysians who are open to change. The people of Vietnam eat the freshest diet of the four countries; just like Thailand and Cambodia, dairy produce plays little part and broths such as Beef pho (page 102) and *Hu tieu* (page 110) are often eaten five times a day.

Walking down the street in Mui Ne I passed by lots of little roadside cafes, inside which were industrious chefs who spent hours preparing their ingredients. I was told this is very typical, and that the Vietnamese can spend up to five hours washing and chopping vegetables for a dish that would then take only five minutes to cook. The Vietnamese live to eat and cook well.

The Vietnamese are also very adventurous eaters; there is really no limit to what they will consume. I was told by someone that if it moves, they eat it. (I discovered this to be true one night at a restaurant in Ho Chi Minh City where the restaurant's speciality was serving every part of a snake.) They like to eat incredibly fresh meat that is slaughtered as close to serving as possible. In the northern city of Hanoi I embraced nose-to-tail cooking, preparing pig cooked seven ways, including using the pig's ears and trotters.

Rice is a major component of the diets of the all the countries I went to, but I have to say that the Vietnamese are masters of using it in more than just in its original form – including as rice noodles or rice paper. I felt incredibly lucky to have met rice farmers in their paddy fields and learn from them how to cook the ultimate rice dish.

My time in Vietnam was inspiring and fascinating; the food there is most certainly fun and different, and it's both flavourful and full of texture – crispy, crunchy, chewy, silky and soft.

It is fair to say that this Great Escape was a journey of epic proportions, and I feel that I have barely touched the surface of some of the many ingredients and cooking techniques that each country has to offer. What I found extraordinary was that very often delicious plates of food are created in kitchens kitted out with no more than one gas hob or a grill. Their one-pot cooking produces endless curries, soups, stir-fries and relishes that are both inspiring and fragrant.

In Southeast Asia they cook with the seasons and with the freshest of ingredients, which is key to the flavour of so many of their dishes. There is little room for some Western foods in their diet, such as cheese, bread, pasta, butter and milk, and so ingredients such as coconut milk and coconut cream feature heavily in this book as they are used instead of dairy products.

This phenomenal journey was made memorable thanks to the people that I met along the way, and this book is a tribute to them. So many complete strangers shared their stories and recipes with me, and for a brief moment in time each and every one of them helped me to understand their lifestyles and passion for food. I am incredibly thankful to them, and grateful that with their help I can bring a taste of their world into our Western kitchens.

Snacks / appetisers

Barbecued scallops with spring-onion oil

Roasted coconut cashew nuts

Tamarind, mint and lemonade cooler

Stir-fried mussels and clams

Thai sweetcorn cakes

Minced pork omelette

Roti babi

Grilled squid with tuk meric

Coconut prawns with a sweet chilli sauce

Beef skewers with a mango and tamarind
  dipping sauce

Cambodian-style smoked fish dip

Curry puffs

Vietnamese fresh spring rolls

Loh bak

Orange and ginger caramelised chicken wings

Chicken satay with peanut sauce

Cambodian aubergine and mushroom dip

Oysters with a Thai dipping sauce

SERVES 4

12 scallops in their
 shells
4–6 tbsp vegetable oil
8–10 spring onions,
 finely chopped
1–2 tsp fish sauce
salt and a pinch of
 ground white pepper
drizzle of chilli oil
2 tbsp crispy shallots
 (see page 266)
2 tbsp crushed roasted
 peanuts
2 Thai red chillies,
 finely sliced, to
 garnish (optional)

Barbecued scallops with spring-onion oil

While I was in Ho Chi Minh City, in Vietnam, I visited Ben Thanh Market with a restaurant owner named Vy. It is the largest market in the city, selling everything from electrical goods and silk to live frogs and dried spices, and is the heart of the community; Vy told me she had been shopping for ingredients twice a day in a market like this since she was a toddler. It was here that I was given the opportunity to cook this scallop dish.

This recipe combines the fragrance of spring onions with the natural sweetness of scallops and the crunchy texture of peanuts to make a delicious and quick appetiser. I cooked this over charcoal, although a grill is fine, but either way it is easy to overcook scallops, so keep an eye on them.

Open the scallops and clean them, removing the roe. Reserve the top shells. (Wash and dry them – you need these to cook the scallops in.)

Place a wok over a high heat and add the oil. Sauté the spring onions for a few minutes to soften, then stir in a dash of fish sauce and the white pepper to taste. Remove the wok from the heat.

Season the scallops with salt and pepper and arrange them in the clean shells. Spoon the spring onion mixture on top of each scallop and drizzle with chilli oil. Place on a grill rack and cook over hot coals for 4–5 minutes or until the scallops caramelise. Alternatively, place the scallop shells on a baking tray and grill for 3–4 minutes under a high heat until cooked.

Serve the scallops in their shells, scattered with crispy shallots and crushed roasted peanuts. Garnish with sliced red chilli, if you wish.

SERVES 4–5
200g cashew nuts
25g butter
1 tbsp sea salt flakes
1 tbsp crushed red
  chilli flakes
50g sweetened
  desiccated coconut,
  toasted

Roasted coconut cashew nuts

I could easily snack on nuts all day long. The mild taste of cashew nuts lends itself to being paired with stronger flavours, which is why I think this dish works so well. Here there is an excellent balance between sweet and spicy.

The nuts take only minutes to prepare and you can apply this recipe to other nuts, too, particularly almonds or peanuts. If you wish, you can make these up to two weeks in advance and keep them in an airtight container.

Preheat the oven to 180°C/Fan 160°C/Gas 4. Place the nuts on an ungreased baking tray and bake for about 10–15 minutes until they are lightly browned.

Meanwhile, melt the butter and place in a medium mixing bowl. Add the salt and chilli flakes and mix well. When the nuts are ready, tip them into the bowl. Toss the nuts, ensuring that they are completely coated in butter. Transfer the nuts to a plate, sprinkle over the coconut and mix well – it won't necessarily stick to the nuts, but it should decorate them.

Serve immediately or allow to cool and store in an airtight container.

Tamarind, mint and lemonade cooler

This recipe is inspired by a very similar drink I was served at a restaurant in Cambodia. The addition of the tamarind makes the drink a little sour, but incredibly refreshing. I also think it would make a great cocktail with a shot of gin or vodka.

Place the tamarind paste in a measuring jug and top it up with the water. Mix well. Pour into a small saucepan set over a medium heat, then add the sugar and mint leaves. Bring to a gentle boil, allowing the flavours to infuse for 4–5 minutes.

Remove from the heat and discard the mint leaves, then add the lime juice. Pour the liquid into a large jug and top up with the cloudy lemonade. Place some ice in four glasses and fill with an equal share of the drink. Decorate with some fresh mint sprigs and drink immediately.

SERVES 4

3 tbsp tamarind paste
100–150ml water
1 tsp caster sugar
large handful of mint leaves, plus extra sprigs to decorate
juice of 1 lime
1 litre cloudy lemonade (preferably sugar-free)
ice cubes, to serve

Stir-fried mussels and clams

For years I have steamed mussels and clams French-style with different wines and herbs, as this is how I was taught to cook them, but Cambodia opened my eyes to a new way of cooking shellfish – stir-frying them. In markets and restaurants I saw clams and mussels being tossed and thrown around woks, and once the shells started to open the flavourings would seep into the meat, making the flesh inside even juicer.

When cooking shellfish, do use the freshest ingredients available and be sure not to eat any seafood whose shells do not open.

Discard any gaping mussels or clams that do not close when the shells are tapped. Place a wok over a medium heat and add the vegetable oil. Sauté the garlic, chilli and shallots for 1 minute, then stir in the chilli paste, palm sugar, oyster sauce, fish sauce and lime juice and sauté for 2–3 minutes to soften.

Add the mussels and clams and bring the mixture to the boil. If you wish, cover with a lid to help the shellfish steam through. Keep moving the shells around the wok – as they begin to open they will soak up the liquid as well as release their own juices. After 6 minutes, the clams and mussels should be cooked, so remove them from the heat, toss in the basil, season, and serve immediately. Discard any mussels or clams that do not open.

SERVES 4 AS A STARTER, 2 AS A MAIN

500g fresh mussels, debearded and cleaned
500g fresh clams, cleaned
2 tbsp vegetable oil
4 garlic cloves, peeled and finely chopped
1 red long finger chilli, thinly sliced
3 shallots, peeled and finely sliced
2 tbsp chilli paste
1–2 tsp palm sugar
1 tbsp oyster sauce
2 tbsp fish sauce
juice of 1 lime
large handful of holy basil, roughly chopped
sea salt and crushed black pepper

Thai sweetcorn cakes

MAKES 8 CAKES

10g cornflour
60g flour
pinch of salt
2 medium eggs
2 tbsp Thai red curry
  paste (see page 102)
250g sweetcorn kernels
2–3 kaffir lime leaves,
  finely shredded
handful of chopped
  coriander
1 tbsp fish sauce
vegetable oil, for
  shallow frying
Thai sweet chilli sauce
  (see page 43), to serve

The best snacks are the ones that you eat more of than you should. I could be categorised as a 'snacker', and when growing up my mum would always tell me off for ruining my appetite. I only tell you this because to me these cakes are one of those snacks; dipped into sweet chilli sauce, one, two or three are never enough. Not only that, they are very easy to make and cook in a matter of minutes.

To prepare the sweetcorn cakes, sift the cornflour, flour and salt into a mixing bowl. Mix well. Add the eggs and curry paste and mix well to form a batter. Add the remaining ingredients (except the oil and chilli sauce) and mix well so that the corn kernels are well coated.

To check the seasoning, fry a little of the mixture in an oiled pan and taste, then adjust the seasoning of the uncooked mixture accordingly, adding a little more salt and/or sugar as necessary.

Heat some oil to the depth of 2–3cm in a deep frying pan or wok and when hot add 2 tablespoons of the mixture. Fry the patties in batches for 1–2 minutes on each side, until golden brown. Drain on a baking tray lined with kitchen paper and keep warm in a low oven while you cook the rest.

When all the sweetcorn cakes are ready, serve immediately with some Thai sweet chilli sauce.

Minced pork omelette

Dee, wife to Gong, who helped us arrange our Thailand trip, recommended this *Kai jiaw moo* as it is their favourite snack. Eggs are commonly used in Thai cuisine, and the Asian influence in this omelette makes it a tasty and filling snack.

It may seem unusual that you add the pork raw, but frying the omelette in the wok over a high heat will cook the mince in minutes; however, you do need to get the oil really hot first. If you prefer, you can subsititute the pork with turkey or chicken.

This omelette is delicious served with a crisp, green, herby salad, but for extra heat offer the Thai chilli sauce alongside.

First make the chilli sauce. Place the oil in a sauté pan set over a medium heat. Add the shallots, garlic and chillies and sauté for 1–2 minutes, to soften. Allow the mixture to cool, then place in a food processor with the remaining ingredients and pulse until smooth. Set aside.

For the omelette, whisk the eggs together in a large mixing bowl then add the minced pork, soy sauce, fish sauce, oyster sauce, white pepper and spring onion. Mix well. Place a wok or frying pan over a medium heat and add the oil. When the oil is hot enough (add ½ teaspoon of the mixture to the pan and if it sizzles straight away, it's ready), add the rest of the mixture. Fry for 2–3 minutes until it is golden brown on the bottom. Turn over the omelette and fry for another 2–3 minutes, until the pork is cooked through.

Remove the omelette from the pan immediately and place on a serving plate. Garnish with the coriander leaves and serve with the chilli sauce alongside.

SERVES 2

OMELETTE
4 large eggs
100g minced pork
1 tsp light soy sauce
½ tsp fish sauce
2 tbsp oyster sauce
½ tsp ground white
  pepper
1 spring onion, finely
  chopped
4 tbsp groundnut or
  vegetable oil

THAI CHILLI SAUCE
2 tbsp vegetable oil
4 shallots, peeled and
  thinly sliced
2 garlic cloves, peeled
  and thinly sliced
2 red bird's eye chillies,
  deseeded and thinly
  sliced
handful of coriander,
  chopped, plus extra
  to serve
juice of 1 lime
1 tsp fish sauce
1 tsp honey, to taste

Roti babi

Deriving from the Nonya cusine of Malaysia, *Roti babi* can be literally translated as pig bread (*roti* meaning bread, *babi* meaning pig) – it is essentially a stuffed pork mince sandwich. It is best made with bread that has been left out overnight to harden, otherwise the sandwich will be too soggy, but if you can't do this, slice the bread and place it in a heated oven for a few minutes to dry it out a little.

There are many versions of this recipe, and in Malaysia crab and cabbage are also added, but for me simplicity is key. Don't be concerned if your mince looks fatty, as you want all the fat to soak into the bread whilst cooking. This is a delicious and different (although admittedly not healthy) approach to the humble sandwich.

Heat 2 tablespoons of oil in a wok over a medium heat and add the shallots and garlic. Stir-fry until translucent, taking care not to burn the garlic. Add the ground spices and white pepper and cook until fragrant – the mixture should now also turn a little dry as the oil is absorbed. Add the soy sauce, water, pork and a pinch of salt and mix well. Stir-fry the pork mince for 4–5 minutes until the pork is cooked. Remove from the heat and allow to cool.

Remove the crusts from the bread and discard. Cut the remaining bread into 5cm thick slices. Taking one slice at a time, cut each one into a 7.5 x 7.5cm square. To create a pocket for the stuffing, lay the trimmed bread flat on a chopping board. Using a small, very sharp knife, make a horizontal slit into the side of the bread, taking care not to go all of the way through. Push about 2 tablespoons of the pork mixture into the pocket and carefully stuff, pressing down the mixture. Repeat this process, using up the remaining bread slices.

Place a frying pan with a thin layer of oil on a medium heat. When the oil is hot, dip one of the stuffed sandwiches into the seasoned egg mixture, making sure the sandwich is evenly coated, then fry it over a low heat until all sides are slightly brown. Remove and drain on kitchen paper while you fry the rest. Cut open and serve immediately.

SERVES 4–6 (MAKES 12 SMALL SANDWICHES)
2 leftover large unsliced sandwich loaves or bloomers
4–5 eggs, beaten and seasoned with sea salt and freshly ground black pepper

STUFFING
vegetable oil, for frying
8 shallots, peeled and finely diced
6 garlic cloves, peeled and crushed
2 tsp ground coriander
2 tsp ground ginger
2 tsp ground nutmeg
½ tsp white pepper
2 tbsp dark sweet soy sauce
2 tbsp water
400g minced pork

SERVES 4

GRILLED SQUID
500–600g whole squid
  (including tentacles),
  cleaned
olive oil, to drizzle
sea salt

TUK MERIC
1 tbsp Kampot
  peppercorns,
  lightly crushed
1 tbsp sea salt
juice of 4 limes

Grilled squid with tuk meric

When squid is cooked to perfection, very little is needed to enhance its natural flavour – except perhaps a Cambodian dipping sauce called *Tuk meric*.

This sauce celebrates one of Cambodia's finest ingredients: Kampot pepper. Grown in the region of the same name, this pepper is regarded as one of the best in the world because of its eucalyptus taste and unique heat. Like many other trades in Cambodia, Kampot-pepper production was greatly affected by the war in the 1960s, but since then locals have worked hard to keep the pepper in production. Although limited quantities of this vegetable translate to a higher price, it is worth every penny.

Kampot pepper is available online and is best bought on the vine and when green in colour – the black and red peppercorns are the dried version and have a more intense flavour. Buying the peppercorns whole gives them a longer shelf life. If you can't get Kampot, use your favourite pepper variety instead.

Wash the squid and pat dry with kitchen paper. Cut off the tentacles and place them in a large bowl. Cut open the bodies and then, using a sharp knife, score them in a criss-cross pattern on the inside. Add these to the bowl with the tentacles, drizzle with olive oil and sprinkle with salt.

Light the barbecue or heat the grill. Make the *tuk meric* dipping sauce before you start cooking the squid. Place all the ingredients in a bowl and mix together to combine. Taste and add more lime juice or pepper, if necessary.

When the barbecue or grill is ready, cook the squid for 30 seconds on each side until opaque and just cooked – do not overcook it or it will become tough and chewy. Cut the pieces in half on the diagonal, if you wish, then transfer to a plate and serve alongside the *tuk meric*.

Coconut prawns with a sweet chilli sauce

Some dishes are naughty but nice – and this is one of them. I was lucky enough to sample some of the best coconut prawns while in the town of Ao Nang in Thailand. On a walk to the main street I passed two women on a large street stall with an array of fried offerings. There was only one item I wanted to try and, for a very reasonable price, six large, fried, coconut prawns were carefully placed in a small plastic bag and the sweet chilli sauce drizzled all over. The desiccated-coconut coating added a delicate sweetness to the overall flavour and extra crunch to the batter. It was hard not to demolish them in seconds.

First make the chilli sauce. Put the sugar and water in a small heavy-based saucepan. Stir to dissolve the sugar, then add the chilli, garlic, fish sauce and vinegar. Bring to the boil and simmer for 8–10 minutes to let the flavours develop and the liquid turn red from the chilli.

After 10 minutes, mix the cornflour with the water in a bowl. Mix well then pour into the chilli sauce. Turn up the heat and allow the sauce to thicken. When it takes on a sticky consistency, remove from the heat, tip the sauce into a bowl and allow to cool.

Place the flour in a bowl with the salt and cayenne pepper. Make a well in the centre and add the beer and egg yolk. Gradually whisk together until you have a smooth batter. Leave to rest for 30 minutes. In a clean bowl, whisk the egg white until it forms stiff peaks. Stir the cold water into the batter and fold in the egg whites.

Heat the oil to 180°C in a large frying pan. (Use a thermometer or test by dropping in a small amount of batter – if it sizzles immediately the oil is ready.) On a tray, spread out the coconut and place bowls with the prawns, flour and batter in a line. Ensure the prawns are dry, but if not, pat them with kitchen paper. Dust the prawns with flour, dip them into the batter, then roll in the coconut. Drop them into the hot oil for 1–2 minutes each side or until golden brown. Remove, drain on kitchen paper, and keep them warm in a low oven while you fry the rest. Serve immediately with the sweet chilli sauce.

SERVES 4

COCONUT PRAWNS
110g plain flour, plus extra for dusting
pinch of salt
½ tsp cayenne pepper
150ml Thai beer
1 egg, separated
50ml water, chilled
150g desiccated coconut
24 medium-sized raw prawns, peeled and tails on
vegetable oil, for deep-frying

SWEET CHILLI SAUCE
2 tbsp caster sugar
500ml water
1 red long finger chilli, deseeded and finely chopped
3 garlic cloves, peeled and finely chopped
1 tbsp fish sauce
1 tbsp rice vinegar
½ tsp cornflour
1–2 tbsp water

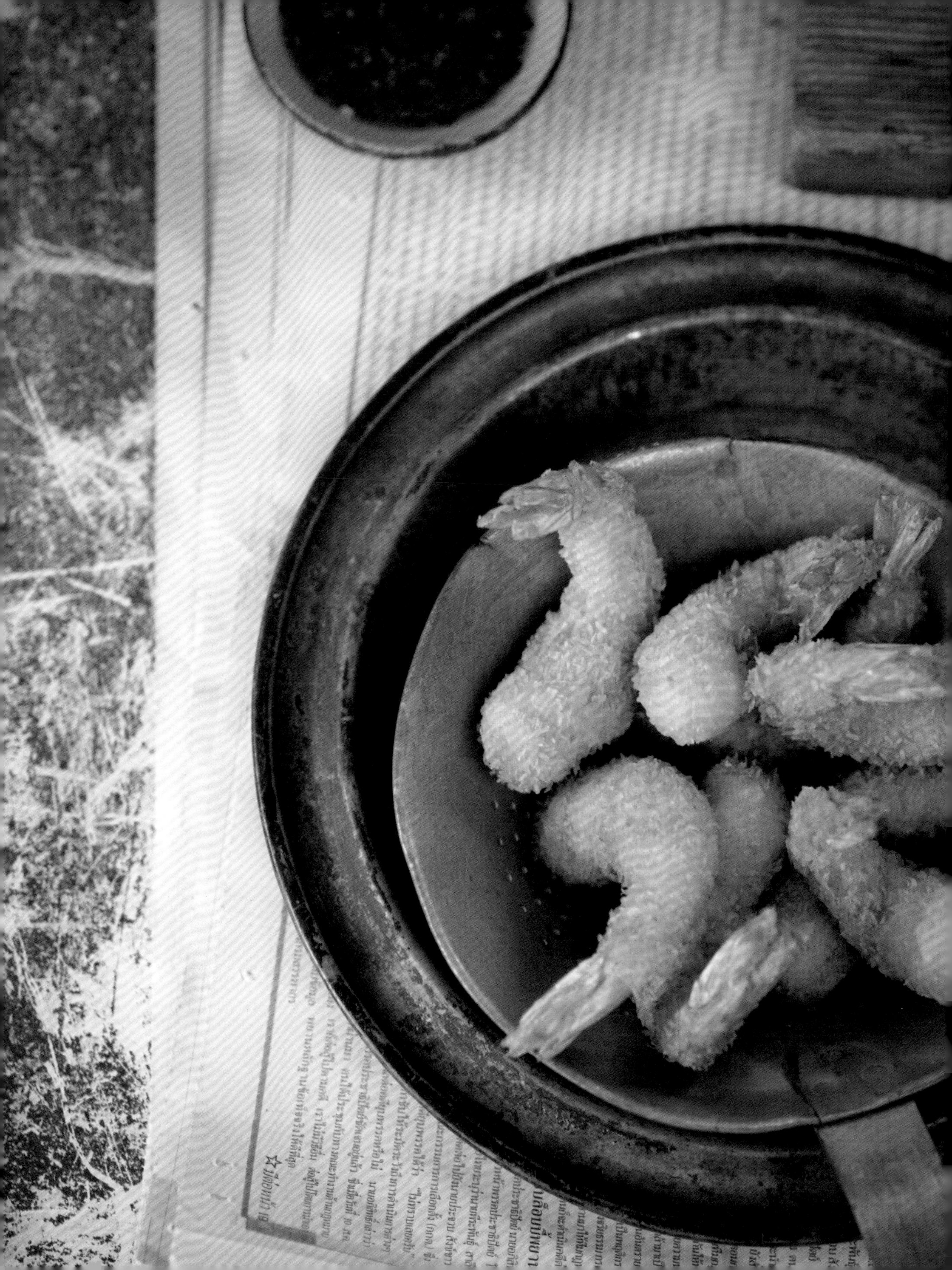

Beef skewers with a mango and tamarind dipping sauce

In Cambodia it was refreshing to go back to basics and cook over charcoal. I love the flavours from an open flame, and beef skewers cooked this way are a particular favourite. The accompanying mango and tamarind dipping sauce has a sweet and sour flavour which is perfect with the juicy, marinated meat.

For extra fragrance and impact, cook the beef on lemongrass skewers. Simply remove the outer woody skin from untrimmed stalks and peel it off to expose the inner stalk.

If using, soak wooden skewers in warm water for at least 30 minutes to prevent them scorching during cooking. Meanwhile, make the marinade. Combine the galangal, garlic, oyster sauce, soy sauce, palm sugar, oil and seasoning in a bowl. Taste and adjust the seasoning if necessary. Add the beef to the marinade and combine well to coat the meat. Cover and place in a refrigerator for 1–3 hours.

Next, prepare the dipping sauce. Place a sauté pan or wok over a medium heat and add the oil. Add the shallots and slowly caramelise them – this should take around 4–5 minutes. Add the ginger and mango and cook for a couple of minutes until the mango starts to break down. Add the chilli paste and mix well, allowing the paste to cook for a minute or so. Add the tamarind paste, fish sauce, honey and water and simmer until most of the liquid has evaporated and it has a thick, syrupy consistency. Remove from the pan and pour into a bowl. Allow to cool. Cover and place in the refrigerator until the beef skewers are ready to be cooked.

Place a griddle pan over a medium heat. Thread the beef pieces onto the skewers and cook on the hot griddle for 2–3 minutes on each side, until the meat is tender. Baste the skewers while cooking. When cooked, remove the beef from the pan, set aside and allow to rest for a few minutes. Repeat this process until all the skewers are cooked. Serve alongside the mango and tamarind dipping sauce.

MAKES 8–10 SKEWERS

BEEF SKEWERS
2.5cm knob of galangal, peeled and crushed
3 garlic cloves, peeled and crushed
1 tbsp oyster sauce
2 tbsp dark soy sauce
1 tsp palm sugar
2 tbsp vegetable oil
sea salt and crushed black pepper
500g beef sirloin, cut into 3cm pieces

MANGO AND TAMARIND DIPPING SAUCE
2 tbsp vegetable oil
2 shallots, peeled and finely diced
2.5cm knob of ginger, peeled and finely chopped
1 ripe mango, peeled and diced
1–2 tsp chilli paste
2 tbsp tamarind paste
½ tsp fish sauce
1–2 tsp honey
approx. 100ml water

SERVES 6–8

100g white fish, such as
  cod or whiting
200g undyed smoked
  haddock
zest and juice of 2 limes
handful of coriander
  stalks, plus leaves,
  finely shredded
pinch of black
  peppercorns
2–3 tbsp vegetable oil
3 garlic cloves, peeled
  and crushed
2 shallots, peeled and
  finely chopped
2cm knob of galangal,
  peeled and crushed
3 small red chillies,
  deseeded and chopped
1 tbsp tamarind paste
25g roasted peanuts,
  lightly crushed
2 tbsp fish sauce
1 tsp prahok (anchovy
  paste)
1 spring onion, sliced
small handful of Thai
  basil, finely shredded

Cambodian-style smoked fish dip

Smoked fish is a common ingredient in Cambodia, as it is does not deteriorate in the endless intense summer heat in a country where most homes do not have a fridge. As well as preserving the fish, smoking adds flavour, and when combined in this dip with peanuts and tamarind it creates an unusual balance between salty, sour and spicy.

By the time the French colonial occupation of Cambodia came to an end, the departing Europeans had firmly left their mark on Cambodian cuisine. This dip is one such example of where the two cuisines meet at a crossroads. The idea is predominantly French, yet the ingredients remain distinctly Cambodian. Like any dip, it is best served with a crusty French baguette or some fresh crudités.

Place all the fish in a pan of simmering water with the lime zest, coriander stalks and peppercorns and poach for 4–5 minutes until cooked through. Remove from the water using a slotted spoon, drain on kitchen paper and allow to cool.

In a frying pan, heat the oil and sauté the garlic, shallots, galangal and chillies for 3–4 minutes until all are softened. Remove from the pan and place in a mixing bowl. Flake the fish into the bowl, discarding the skin, add the remaining ingredients and mix well. Alternatively, transfer the mixture to a food processor and blend together for a smooth texture.

Taste and season if necessary, remembering that little salt should be required because of the fish ingredients. Serve with fresh, raw vegetables, such as green beans, cucumber and carrots.

Curry puffs

My first experience of these curry puffs, or *Kari paps,* was at a Malaysian version of a service station, where you could help yourself to as many as you wanted and then confess to how many you had eaten when the time came to pay! I admitted to having eaten no less than two and definitely no more than five. They were incredibly moreish.

I would describe this snack as a hybrid; the outside of a Cornish pasty with the filling of a samosa. For all those I spoke to, curry puffs evoked fond childhood memories of eagerly awaiting the day when batches were cooked, and the drifting smell from the oven as the dough turned golden brown and the filling softened and spiced in the pockets. This is a great snack for all the family.

To make the dough, combine the flour and salt in a large bowl. Make a well in the centre and add the melted butter and 5 tablespoons of warm water. Mix with a round-bladed knife to form a dough, adding a little more water if the mixture seems too dry. Tip onto a lightly floured surface and knead for 5–10 minutes to a smooth dough. Cover with cling film and leave to rest in a cool place for 30 minutes.

Meanwhile, prepare the filling. Add the oil to the wok and heat through, stir-fry the garlic and ginger for about 1 minute, until fragrant. Add the onion and fry for 2–3 minutes, until slightly caramelised. Add both types of potato, curry powder, remaining spices and seasoning and cook for 2–3 minutes, so the spices cook through. Pour in the stock and simmer gently for 6–8 minutes or until the liquid has reduced. Remove from the heat and set aside to cool. When completely cool, add the coriander. Adjust the seasoning if necessary.

Preheat the oven to 200°C/Fan 180°C/Gas 6. On a floured work surface, roll out the dough into a log 5–6cm thick. Cut into 1cm slices and roll each log into a small, round pasty. Fill each with 1 tablespoon of filling. Brush the pasty edges with egg yolk and fold over the filling. Press the sides together with a fork to seal. Arrange the puffs on a greased baking sheet, brush with more egg yolk and bake for 25–30 minutes. These are best served warm.

MAKES 18–20

DOUGH
225g plain flour, plus extra for dusting
pinch of salt
60g melted butter
warm water

FILLING
2 tbsp vegetable oil
1 garlic clove, peeled and crushed
2cm knob of ginger, peeled and grated
1 small red onion, peeled and finely chopped
1 small sweet potato, peeled and cut into 1cm dice, then blanched
1 small potato, peeled and cut into 1cm dice, then blanched
1 tbsp curry powder
pinch of ground cumin
pinch of chilli powder
½ tsp sea salt
¼ tsp ground white pepper
200ml vegetable stock
small handful of coriander, finely chopped
2 egg yolks, to finish

Vietnamese fresh spring rolls

MAKES 12

PORK
2 tbsp sesame oil
1 tsp Chinese five-spice
salt and freshly ground
  black pepper
300g pork tenderloin
  fillet, sinew removed
  and finely sliced
vegetable oil, for frying

DRESSING
juice of 1 lime
1 tsp fish sauce
1 tsp rice vinegar
1 tsp caster sugar

In my opinion, the *Nem cuon mua xuan*, or fresh spring roll, sums up Vietnamese food: fresh, healthy, textural and balanced in flavour. On my travels I discovered that Vietnamese chefs can study for months learning how to make these rolls, being taught the different filling and dipping sauce combinations. Like many dishes in Vietnam, the ingredients in spring rolls vary from region to region and throughout the seasons. The chefs that I worked with in Hanoi described these as 'summer spring rolls'.

On my last night in Vietnam I served these spring rolls as the first of seven courses. They work perfectly as an appetiser and look pretty impressive, too. For the best results you need to use the freshest ingredients. For extra crunch I have used baby gem lettuce, however, follow your palate to chop and change the ingredients in the rolls, such as using crab instead of the prawns, changing the pork for mushrooms or, if you don't like rice noodles, add more lettuce and cucumber. The hoisin peanut dipping sauce is one of the most commonly served accompaniments to these rolls.

SPRING ROLL

1 baby gem lettuce,
   washed, core removed
   and shredded
handful of coriander
   leaves, torn
12 sheets of rice paper,
   16cm in diameter
small handful of Thai
   basil, picked
small handful of saw
   leaf or mint leaves,
   picked
small handful of
   coriander leaves,
   picked
200g cooked rice
   vermicelli noodles
12 chive flowers
12 cooked prawns,
   peeled, de-veined and
   cut in half lengthways

DIPPING SAUCE

1 garlic clove, peeled
   and finely chopped
1 red Thai chilli, finely
   chopped
3 tbsp hoisin sauce
2 tbsp fish sauce
1 tbsp caster sugar
2 tbsp crunchy peanut
   butter
4–6 tbsp coconut milk
1 tbsp tamarind paste
100–150ml water
1 tbsp dark soy sauce

For the pork, mix together the sesame oil, five-spice and salt and pepper in a bowl. Add the pork strips and toss together to coat. Heat a little vegetable oil in a frying pan and stir-fry the pork strips for 2–3 minutes, until cooked through. Remove from the heat and set aside to cool.

To make the dressing, whisk together all the ingredients in a large bowl to combine. Add the shredded baby gem and coriander leaves and coat well in the dressing.

Fill a large bowl with warm water and, one at a time, quickly dip in each sheet of rice paper, passing them through but not soaking them. Drain them flat on a clean, damp cloth. Do not over-soak or they will fall apart and tear when being rolled.

To make the dipping sauce, gently fry the garlic and chilli in a little oil in a frying pan for 2 minutes until softened. Add the remaining ingredients and simmer for 6–8 minutes until reduced by half, adding extra water if needed to loosen the sauce.

To make the rolls, lay all your ingredients in an assembly line. Take one rice paper sheet and lay it flat on a clean surface. Place the herbs on top and gently create a small pile of rice noodles on top (the pile should be long and narrow). Fold over two sides of the rice paper to enclose the filling and roll over once. Place the chive flower alongside the rolled up section. Take one strip of pork and two halves of prawn and lay them neatly alongside the chive flower – they should be positioned tightly against the roll. Slowly roll once again. Tuck the edge of the rice paper into the filling. To seal the roll, lightly brush the rice paper with warm water. (Make sure the filling is compact.) The prawn and spring onion should be visible through the rice paper. Repeat the process with the remaining sheets of rice paper. Cover with cling film to stop the rolls drying out.

Serve with the dipping sauce.

Loh bak

Loh bak is the Malay version of a sausage; lean pork is marinated in a mixture of ingredients, including Chinese five-spice, water chestnuts and carrots, then encased in a bean-curd skin. This dish originated from Eastern China, where it was known as *Ngoh hiang*, but as Nonya cuisine evolved, this dish soon found itself served at the meals of festival celebrations such as Chinese New Year. To me this dish is a snack, but in Malaysia many eat this as a main meal.

The bean-curd skins create a delicious crunchy exterior and can be found at any good Chinese supermarket. An easy but slightly different substitute for bean-curd skins would be filo pastry – just layer the filo with melted butter in between and place the pork mixture in the middle. Serve with a chilli sauce, as they do in Malaysia (see page 37).

Place the pork in a large mixing bowl and add all the other ingredients except the bean-curd sheets, cornflour, oil and cucumber. Cover with cling film and leave to marinate for 1 hour.

Divide the mixture between the bean curd rectangles, fold in the two short sides and roll from the long sides, making sure you roll tightly. Seal the skins with the cornflour mixture.

Heat the oil in a deep pan or wok for deep-frying. When it is hot enough, fry the seasoned meat rolls for 4–5 minutes until golden brown and cooked through. Remove the rolls with a slotted spoon and drain to remove any excess oil.

Slice the *loh bak* and serve with sliced cucumber and sweet chilli sauce (see page 43).

MAKES APPROXIMATELY 8–10 PORK ROLLS

500g lean pork fillet, cut into strips
75g water chestnuts, skinned and finely chopped
3 garlic cloves, peeled and finely chopped
1 small onion, peeled and finely chopped
1 small turnip, peeled and finely chopped
1 small carrot, peeled and finely chopped
4 tbsp oyster sauce
1 tbsp dark soy sauce
½ tsp ground white pepper
1 tbsp sugar
2 tsp Chinese five-spice powder
1 egg, beaten
8–10 bean curd sheets, cut into 15 x 20cm rectangles
1 tsp cornflour mixed with 1 tbsp cold water
vegetable oil, for deep-frying
sliced cucumber, to serve

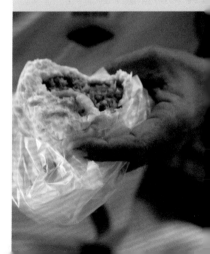

Orange and ginger caramelised chicken wings

SERVES 4
vegetable oil, for
  cooking
6–8 shallots, peeled
  and sliced
4 garlic cloves, peeled
  and sliced
2 lemongrass stalks,
  trimmed and bashed
5cm knob of fresh
  ginger, peeled and
  julienned
zest and juice of
  2 oranges
150g granulated sugar
160ml water
2 tbsp fish sauce
1kg chicken wings
sea salt and crushed
  black pepper

Not only are chicken wings packed with flavour, because the meat cooks on the bone, but they are also great value for money. Chicken wings are the ultimate snack and I think they should only be eaten with fingers – with a napkin on standby.

The base of this dish is a caramel sauce, which is incredibly easy to prepare. Such sauces are the cornerstone of Vietnamese cuisine and, surprisingly, are mainly used in savoury dishes. For this recipe the caramel sauce is a great cheat to help the chicken wings take on a dark golden-brown colour; the orange adds a bitter sweetness and the ginger a little spicy kick.

Preheat the oven to 180°C/Fan 160°C/Gas 4. Heat the oil in a pan and add the shallots, garlic, lemongrass, ginger and orange zest and cook for 2–3 minutes, until the ingredients have softened. Add the sugar, water, orange juice and fish sauce and allow to dissolve. Cook until the mixture has reduced and thickened. This should take 3–4 minutes and the sauce should start turning syrupy. Remove from the heat and set aside.

To prepare the chicken, place a large frying pan over a high heat and add 3–4 tablespoons of vegetable oil. Season the chicken, then, in batches, sear the pieces for 3 minutes, until browned. Add the chicken wings to an ovenproof dish and pour over the caramel sauce, mixing well to coat. Cook in the oven for 40–45 minutes until golden brown and sticky. Halfway through cooking, baste the chicken wings.

Remove the chicken wings from the oven, season with sea salt and crushed black pepper and serve with the sauce spooned over.

❧

Chicken satay with peanut sauce

SERVES 4–6 (MAKES
APPROX. 14–16 SKEWERS)

SATAY

500g chicken thighs,
    skinned and deboned
3 shallots, peeled and
    coarsely chopped
2 garlic cloves, peeled
    and coarsely chopped
3cm knob of galangal,
    peeled and grated
2 lemongrass stalks,
    trimmed and white
    part finely chopped
1cm knob of turmeric
    root, peeled, or 1 tsp
    ground turmeric
1 tbsp ground coriander
1 tsp ground cumin
1 tsp sea salt
1 tsp palm sugar or dark
    brown sugar
pinch of freshly ground
    black pepper
1 tsp fish sauce
½ chilli, deseeded and
    chopped
4 tbsp peanut oil
vegetable or groundnut
    oil, for brushing

Originally an Indonesian dish, satay is now cooked all over Asia. Each Southeast Asian country has its own adaptation, but for me the Malay version is one of the best.

One lunchtime, as I parked my car in Penang, I discovered an amazing satay stall. Drifting over was the smell of the chicken sizzling on the hot coals, the distinctive marinade with its spices being charred. In the corner next to the grill, a sizeable tub of peanut sauce was eagerly waiting to be dipped into. I was left with little choice but to tuck in – and it didn't disappoint. The ladies on the stall told me that satay used to be served at special occasions, but now it's an everyday food.

To achieve the best flavour you should only use meat off the bone. Marinating is key; the meat needs to be left for at least 12 hours for a more developed flavour. I would recommend barbecuing the skewers to get that smoky flavour, but you can also use a grill or a griddle pan. You can substitute the chicken for pork, beef or even prawns.

Slice the chicken into thin strips. Grind together the shallots, garlic, galangal, lemongrass, turmeric and the remaining spices in a food processor or a pestle and mortar until you have a rough paste. Taste and adjust the seasoning with salt, sugar and pepper. Add the fish sauce and chilli and combine. Mix the paste with the peanut oil and add to the chicken, tossing to coat well. Cover with cling film and leave to marinate in the fridge overnight, to allow all the various flavours to develop.

Soak 16 bamboo skewers (approximately 15cm long) in warm water (this will prevent them scorching) half an hour before you are ready to cook the chicken. When you are ready, thread the marinated chicken onto the skewers until they are three-quarters full, but be careful not to overcrowd each skewer.

Brush the griddle pan with oil. Allow the griddle pan to get very hot and, when ready, gently lay the satay sticks onto it. Baste the chicken with oil occasionally during cooking. Grill the chicken until it has

MALAYSIAN PEANUT SAUCE

2 tbsp vegetable oil

1 shallot, peeled and
   finely diced

1 red chilli (deseeded, if
   you prefer)

1 tbsp crushed garlic

1 tbsp crushed ginger

4 tbsp crunchy peanut
   butter

1 tsp tamarind paste

1 tsp dark sweet
   soy sauce

100ml coconut cream

50ml water

cooked through and has begun to pick up a few crispy brown-black spots, about 5–7 minutes, turning frequently. If you are cooking the satay sticks on the barbecue the time may vary depending on how hot the coals are.

For the satay sauce, place a saucepan over a medium heat. Add the oil followed by the shallot, chilli, garlic and ginger. Sauté for 2–3 minutes until the shallots are softened and the oil begins to take on the red colour of the chilli. Add in the peanut butter and stir, breaking it down. It should start to melt. Now add the tamarind paste and dark soy sauce and stir well. Pour the coconut cream and water into the saucepan and stir for 3–4 minutes, until the peanut butter has been incorporated into the satay sauce. Simmer the mixture on a low heat for around 1–2 minutes, then turn off the heat. Serve warm with the chicken skewers.

Cambodian aubergine and mushroom dip

Raw aubergines and mushrooms share one characteristic, in that their flesh is like a sponge and so beautifully absorbs other flavours during cooking. Here the Cambodian flavours of tamarind, Thai basil, garlic and chilli mesh together to create a delicious and slightly unusual dip.

There are a wide variety of aubergines and mushrooms available, but for this I would recommend using large aubergines, because these will provide the most flesh. For the mixed mushrooms, choose those with a deep woody flavour, such as oyster, chestnut and crimini.

Place the aubergines on an open gas flame and chargrill them for 25–30 minutes, turning frequently, until charred and softened.

Allow the dried mushrooms to sit in enough hot water to cover them for 20 minutes. When the mushrooms have doubled in size, drain them, reserving the liquid as you will need this later.

Heat some oil in a wide frying pan over a high heat and add the shallots, garlic and chilli and sauté for 2–3 minutes to soften. Add all the mushrooms, season with salt and pepper and sauté over a high heat until golden brown and any moisture coming out of the mushrooms has been cooked off. Add the fish sauce, palm sugar and tamarind paste and fry with the other ingredients for 1 minute.

Place the mushroom mixture into a food processor. Scrape out the flesh from the aubergines and add to the processor. If necessary, add a splash of the dried mushroom soaking liquid and pulse until combined, but do not over-process as the dip should still have some texture.

Place the dip in a bowl and garnish with some shredded Thai basil leaves and serve with some crusty bread or chopped raw vegetables.

SERVES 4–6

2 large aubergines
10g dried shiitake
  mushrooms, soaked
  in hot water
2 tbsp vegetable oil
2 shallots, peeled
  and sliced
2 garlic cloves, peeled
  and crushed
1 red chilli, thinly sliced
  (deseeded, if you
  prefer)
150g fresh mixed
  mushrooms
sea salt and freshly
  ground black pepper
1 tsp fish sauce
1 tbsp palm sugar
1 tbsp tamarind paste
handful of Thai basil
  leaves, shredded
crusty French baguette
  or chopped raw
  vegetables, to serve

Oysters with a Thai dipping sauce

I discovered this dish in the Southern Thai region of Khlong Thom while being taken oyster diving by a local fisherman, Sard. Such was Sard's success at catching oysters that he was able to not only support his family in this way, but also his brother's and sister's family too.

In the Western world oysters are considered a delicacy, but Sard and his family dined every day on some of the largest oysters I have ever seen. Children as young as 4 years old were tucking in, spooning this sauce on top and swallowing them whole. It was amazing to see.

This dipping sauce provides a refreshing change alongside oysters, without overpowering their delicate and unique flavour. However, if you don't like your oysters raw, this sauce is ideal for baking them with; simply place the oysters in their shells in a hot oven (200°C/Fan 180°C/Gas 6), spoon over the sauce and bake for 10–15 minutes or until cooked. Typically this dish is served with extra slices of garlic and chilli.

If you wish you can spread a thick layer of rock salt on one or two serving platters and scatter over the seaweed on which to sit the oysters in their half shells.

In a bowl, mix together the garlic, shallot, coriander and chilli for the dipping sauce. Stir well. Add the sugar, soy sauce, fish sauce and lime juice to the mixture and mix well.

When ready to serve, spoon half the sauce over the oysters and put the rest into a small bowl to serve alongside.

SERVES 4

rock salt and fresh seaweed, to serve (optional)

12 oysters, shucked and lower shells saved

THAI DIPPING SAUCE

3 garlic cloves, peeled and roughly chopped

1 shallot, peeled and roughly chopped

handful of coriander stalks and leaves, roughly chopped

1 Thai red chilli, roughly chopped (deseeded, if you prefer)

1 tbsp sugar

1 tbsp light soy sauce

1 tsp fish sauce

juice of 2 limes

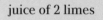

Salads

SERVES 6 AS A STARTER, 4 AS A MAIN

SALAD
500g centre-cut beef
   fillet piece
½ cucumber, sliced
100g green beans,
   cooked and sliced into
   3cm lengths
5 radishes, thinly sliced
1 red pepper, thinly
   sliced
small handful of Thai
   basil leaves
small handful of mint
1 shallot, peeled and
   thinly sliced
2 tbsp crushed roasted
   peanuts
1 red chilli, thinly sliced
1 round head of lettuce,
   leaves torn

MARINADE
1 garlic clove, peeled
   and finely chopped
1–2 tbsp fish sauce
juice of 3 limes, zest of 1
1 tbsp palm sugar
1 lemongrass stalk,
   trimmed and
   thinly sliced

DRESSING
½ tbsp honey
1 tbsp fish sauce
2 tbsp rice vinegar
juice of 1 lime

Cured beef salad

One thing I loved about Cambodia was that the food endlessly surprised me, and this salad was one such dish. It felt modern and chic and proved that their cuisine is once more evolving and moving forward.

It is the preparation of the beef that makes this dish different. The beef is cured by the lime juice in the marinade, making the meat tender and packed with a sour but tangy punch. Whether you serve the beef rare or cooked, it is well worth spending money on a good-quality aged fillet. It really will make a difference. I have added some green beans and radishes here to make the salad more substantial and colourful.

Trim the beef fillet or get a butcher to do it. You only want the eye of the fillet, so if you're trimming it yourself, remove the extra flap of meat that will be attached on one side. (Don't throw it away though – bash it out a bit and it'll make a good steak sandwich.) Cover the beef in cling film and place it in the freezer. This will firm up the beef and make it easier to slice. After 30 minutes, remove the beef from the freezer, take off the cling film and thinly slice the meat against the grain. Cut the slices into thin strips.

To make the marinade, combine all the ingredients in a bowl and mix well. Add the beef, cover with cling film and marinate in the fridge for 30 minutes. When the beef is cured, remove it from the marinade, discarding the liquid.

Make the dressing by combining all the ingredients in a bowl.

In a large salad bowl, combine the beef with all the salad ingredients and mix well. Drizzle the salad with the dressing and toss to coat. Serve immediately.

Kerabu mushroom and chicken salad

This is an unusual dish, compared to what we have come to expect of salads in the Western world, but that's the charm of Malaysia: the mix of cultures living side by side creates some inspiring food. Although essentially Malaysian in style, this salad has influences from Thai cuisine.

There are many different variations of a *Kerabu*, but the flavours must always be balanced between sweet, sour, spicy and salty. This particular version can be considered Nonya because of the Chinese influence of the *Bok nee* – Chinese black fungus – however, you can use any dried fungus for this recipe. This is a substantial salad, best served as a main course with steamed rice, as it is in Malaysia.

Bring the stock to a boil in a medium pan and add the chicken so that it is submerged. Cover the pan and bring back to the boil. Lower the heat and allow to simmer for 12 minutes, until the chicken is cooked through, then remove from the heat and allow to cool slightly. When the chicken is cool to the touch, pull apart to shred and set aside.

Put the fungus in a bowl and cover with boiling water for 10 minutes. Remove from the liquid and thinly slice. Set aside. Dry-fry the coconut until toasted and fragrant.

Make the dressing by mixing together all the ingredients. Set aside.

To make the salad, put the chicken, fungus, coconut and remaining salad ingredients in a bowl. Mix well.

Pour over the dressing and toss all the ingredients until they are evenly covered. Serve immediately.

SERVES 6–8

SALAD
1.5 litres chicken stock
2 skinless chicken breasts
50g dried black fungus
3 tbsp sweetened desiccated coconut
½ green cabbage, finely shredded
2 shallots, peeled and thinly sliced
2 spring onions, thinly sliced
1 red chilli, thinly sliced
small handful of coriander leaves
small handful of mint leaves
2cm knob of ginger, peeled and finely diced

DRESSING
4 tbsp sambal belacan (see page 266)
juice of 2 limes
1–2 tbsp palm sugar
pinch of salt

SERVES 6

1 lemongrass stalk,
  soft white part only,
  thinly sliced
350g cooked jasmine
  rice
1 small pomelo, peeled
  and shredded
2 spring onions, finely
  chopped
1 carrot, grated
1 courgette, grated
100g fine beans, thinly
  sliced
small handful of
  coriander leaves,
  finely shredded
50g beansprouts
100g desiccated
  coconut, toasted
2 Thai red chillies,
  thinly sliced, to serve
small handful of sweet
  basil leaves, shredded,
  to serve

DRESSING

4 tbsp fish sauce
2 tbsp palm sugar
juice of 4 limes
1 red chilli, deseeded
  and finely chopped

Southern Thai rice and pomelo salad

In Southern Thailand this salad is known as *Kao yum*, and it was there that I discovered it. While visiting a local food competition I stepped away to look round the stalls, and on one an amazing array of ingredients was laid out – including rice and shredded pomelo flesh. Intrigued, I stood and watched as the woman on the stall simply mixed a little of all the ingredients from the platter, including the pomelo, into a bowl with some rice and spooned over a dressing. There it was – the *Kao yum*.

A pomelo is one of the largest of the citrus fruits and is native to Southeast Asia; its closest relation is the grapefruit, but its flesh is sweet and firmer. It is worth the time that it takes to peel away the thick skin and pith, as the first taste of this fruit reminds me why I should eat it more often.

This dish is a great way to use up leftover rice, or you can cook it fresh. It is perfect eaten by itself or makes an exciting addition to a picnic.

To prepare the dressing, place all the ingredients in a bowl and mix. Cover with cling film and set aside.

In a pestle and mortar, pound the lemongrass stalk to bruise it slightly but not crush it. Place in a bowl and mix in all the other salad ingredients. Spoon over the dressing and mix again.

When ready to serve, spoon out the rice salad into serving bowls and garnish with the chillies and Thai basil.

Green papaya salad

For me, this salad has the wow factor. The secret to a great *Som tam,* or green papaya salad, is gently mashing the ingredients together in a pestle and mortar so that the juices and flavours are extracted and brought together at the same time. This salad is available all over Thailand – from street corners to upmarket restaurants – and while on my escape round the country a day didn't go by without me eating this salad. In the humidity, the sweet and sour flavours were really refreshing.

Green papaya is a tropical fruit eaten when the flesh is unripe. It is ideal for a salad because at this stage the fruit is slightly bitter and the flesh is firmer. Green papaya is hard to substitute because of its unique taste, but it also isn't the easiest of fruits to get hold of, so if you can't find it I would recommend using a ripe papaya.

In a large pestle and mortar, pound the garlic then add the lime juice, fish sauce, palm sugar and salt. Pound together well. Add the peanuts and lightly crush them, then transfer to a bowl.

Add the beans and beansprouts to the mortar with the shallot, papaya, tomatoes, chilli and ground shrimp and pound until the tomatoes start to break down and the ingredients are mixed together. If you don't have a large enough pestle and mortar, mash the ingredients in batches and place in a mixing bowl, mixing them together at the end.

Remove from the pestle and mortar and add to the ingredients in the bowl. Garnish with the coriander leaves and serve.

SERVES 4

1 garlic clove, peeled
juice of 2 limes
1 tbsp fish sauce
1 tsp palm sugar
pinch of salt
2 tbsp roasted peanuts
100g snake beans or
  green beans, cut into
  3cm lengths
50g beansprouts
1 shallot, peeled and
  thinly sliced
1 green papaya, peeled
  and julienned thinly
  (ideally) on a
  mandolin
2 tomatoes, diced
1 red chilli, deseeded
  and thinly sliced
1 tbsp ground dried
  shrimp

GARNISH
small handful of
  coriander leaves

Malay fruit rojak

There are many different variations of this recipe in Indonesia and the numerous regions of Malaysia. The word *rojak* means mixture, and a chef told me it is so-called because everything but the kitchen sink is thrown into a bowl and tossed together to make a salad. Although this is a fruit-based salad, it is unquestionably a savoury dish. If an initial glance at all the ingredients makes you want to turn the page, please don't; I promise this dish is very fresh, addictive and incredibly light.

Place a wok over a medium heat and fill it with 5cm of oil. When the oil is hot, carefully add the tofu pieces and deep-fry them for 30–45 seconds until lightly puffed up and golden brown. Remove with a slotted spoon and drain on kitchen paper. Continue to cook the tofu in batches until all the chunks are cooked.

Combine all the dressing ingredients and mix well. Season to taste.

In a large bowl, add the tofu to all the other salad ingredients and pour over the dressing. Toss well to coat, then serve.

SERVES 4–6

SALAD
vegetable oil, for deep-frying
100g medium-firm tofu, cut into large chunks
1 small jicama or daikon radish, peeled and cut into large dice
100g beansprouts, washed
½ cucumber, cut into large chunks
½ small pineapple, peeled, cored and cut into large chunks
1 pear, cored and cut into large chunks
50g spinach leaves
70g roasted peanuts, ground
2 shallots, peeled and thinly sliced

DRESSING
10 mint leaves, shredded
juice and zest of 2 limes
2 tbsp granulated sugar
1 tsp honey
1–2 red chillies, finely chopped
2 tbsp water

Roasted duck leg and bamboo shoot salad

A popular dish at one of my restaurants is the Asian duck salad. Once, we took it off the menu and the customers complained, so for years it has kept its place. The demand for such a salad inspired this variation, which is my take on the classic Vietnamese duck and bamboo shoot soup.

I am a big fan of duck, especially the legs as they have a rich gamey flavour and when roasted to perfection the crispy skin is just amazing. In this recipe duck legs are marinated with fresh bamboo shoots, cucumber, spinach and mint, but I couldn't help adding some orange as a nod to the French connection to Vietnam, and the fact that the Vietnamese have soaked up many classic techniques of French cuisine. This makes an impressive and substantial main course.

Preheat the oven to 200°C/Fan 180°C/Gas 6. Pat dry the duck legs with kitchen paper and, using the tip of a sharp knife, lightly score the leg (this will help the fat of the duck render down during roasting). Sprinkle the duck with the cinnamon, five-spice powder, salt and pepper and then rub this into the fat. Place the duck legs skin-side up on a roasting rack, with a pan underneath to catch the fat. Cook for 1 hour; check every 15–20 minutes and baste the duck throughout.

Meanwhile, mix together the orange juice, hoisin sauce, fish sauce, honey, ginger and garlic in a bowl. Once the duck has cooked for an hour, remove from the oven and pour half the marinade over the duck legs (reserving the remainder for later). Return to the oven and continue to cook for a further 15–20 minutes. Once the skin has turned golden brown and crispy, remove the legs from the oven and allow to cool. The meat should be tender and almost falling off the bone.

To prepare the salad, cut the cucumber lengthways into long wide strips using a swivel vegetable peeler, avoiding the seeds in the middle. Mix together the cucumber and remaining salad ingredients and divide amongst four plates.

Using a fork, shred the duck meat, gently pulling it away from the bone and keeping the skin attached to the meat shreds. On the individual plates carefully place meat from each leg on the salad, sprinkle with the sesame seeds and garnish with the crispy shallots.

Finally, make the dressing by placing the reserved marinade in a small saucepan and simmer for a few minutes, until slightly thickened. Cool, then drizzle over the salad. Serve immediately.

SERVES 4

DUCK
4 duck legs, fat trimmed
2 tsp cinnamon
2 tsp Chinese five-spice powder
salt and freshly ground black pepper

MARINADE AND DRESSING
juice of 4 oranges
4 tbsp hoisin sauce
4 tbsp fish sauce
4 tbsp honey
4 tbsp minced ginger
4 garlic cloves, peeled and minced

SALAD
½ cucumber, peeled
130g sliced bamboo shoots, thinly sliced
small handful of mint
50g spinach leaves, washed
50g watercress, washed
2 spring onions, thinly sliced
1 red chilli, deseeded and thinly sliced
2 oranges, peeled and segmented

GARNISH
2 tbsp toasted sesame seeds
4 tsp crispy shallots (see page 266)

SERVES 4 AS A STARTER

8 raw king prawns,
  peeled and de-veined
1 lemongrass stalk
2 tbsp tamarind paste
2cm knob of galangal,
  peeled and sliced
1 green mango, peeled
  and julienned
1 shallot, peeled and
  thinly sliced
1 green and 1 red
  pepper, thinly sliced
1 small carrot, peeled
  and julienned
1 small white daikon
  radish, peeled and
  thinly sliced
small handful of saw
  leaf or spearmint and
  of Thai basil
4 banana flower leaves,
  washed (optional),
  to serve
50g dry roasted
  peanuts, chopped,
  to serve

DRESSING

2 tbsp fish sauce
1 tbsp honey
juice of 1 lime
1 garlic clove, peeled
  and diced
1 red chilli, deseeded
  and finely chopped
pinch of salt
1 tbsp palm or rice
  vinegar
3 tbsp hot water

Green mango salad with king prawns

At the end of my journey around Cambodia I cooked a three-course meal for some of the people who had helped and inspired me during my stay. I wanted to cook them something delicious, but I also wanted to show them that I had learnt a lot about Cambodian cuisine during my travels, so this salad was an obvious choice; a perfect example of authentic Cambodian cuisine.

On the guest list were three members of royalty, and there is no better way to elevate a dish than with the inclusion of king prawns poached in an aromatic broth. The sweet juicy prawns marry perfectly with the slightly tart flesh of the green mango. For a bit of wow factor, I served the salad in purple banana flower leaves to add a vibrant backdrop to the dish.

Place a saucepan over a medium heat and fill with enough water to cover the prawns. Trim and bruise the lemongrass and add along with the tamarind paste and galangal and cook briefly to infuse. Poach the prawns in the infused water for 2–3 minutes until cooked. When cooked, plunge the prawns into some ice to stop them cooking, then set aside.

Combine all the other salad ingredients except the banana flower leaves and the peanuts.

To make the dressing, combine all the ingredients. Taste and adjust the balance and add a little seasoning.

Toss the salad in the dressing. If using a banana flower leaf, turn it inside out, place on a plate and spoon the salad inside. Cut the prawns in half horizontally and place them on top of the salad, then garnish it with the peanuts. Drizzle over the dressing and serve immediately.

Crispy chicken lettuce cups

This is an incredibly tasty salad that I discovered on a street stall in Southern Thailand. The stall was labelled with a tiny piece of paper advertising 'Spicy Chicken'. Around 50 pence later I was handed a paper bowl and was sampling the wares. It struck me that perhaps this dish should have been labelled 'Crispy Spicy Chicken', as it was breaded and also dusted in crunchy white flakes. I was shown a little recycled coffee jar which had ground rice powder inside it, which was an exciting discovery for me. As it turns out, this is a common ingredient in Thailand; it's well worth making and adding to your storecupboard as it adds a really earthy flavour and texture to a dish.

The meat can be a meal in itself, served with a few large crispy lettuce leaves for extra crunch, but I thought the chicken would lend itself to being spooned into little lettuce cups. Dress the salad as close to serving as possible, otherwise the crispy breading will turn soggy.

Cut the chicken breasts in half horizontally. Mix the breadcrumbs with salt and pepper. Press both sides of each chicken strip into the flour and shake off any excess. Dip them into the eggs then press into the breadcrumb mix on both sides. Repeat this twice, if necessary, to get an even coating. Heat the oil in a wide pan and fry the breaded chicken over a high heat for 3–4 minutes on each side until golden brown and cooked through. (Do this in two batches if your pan is not wide enough.) Allow the chicken to cool then cut it into small cubes.

Meanwhile, place the shallots, cucumber, basil and coriander leaves and fresh chillies in the bottom of a large bowl. In another bowl, make the dressing by whisking together all the ingredients to combine. Add the chilli powder, chicken and ground rice powder to the salad and mix well so that the chicken is evenly coated.

Lay the baby gem lettuce leaves on a serving plate and scoop a little of the mixture into each of the leaves. Add the dressing to the salad, toss well to coat evenly, then serve immediately.

SERVES 4

CHICKEN
2 skinless, boneless chicken breasts
100g Panko breadcrumbs (or use natural breadcrumbs)
salt and freshly ground black pepper
50g flour
3 eggs, beaten
4–6 tbsp vegetable oil

SALAD
2 shallots, peeled and finely sliced
½ cucumber, peeled and finely diced
handful of Thai basil leaves
handful of coriander leaves
1 red chilli, deseeded and thinly sliced
1 green chilli, deseeded and thinly sliced
½–1 tsp chilli powder
4 tbsp ground rice powder (see page 266)
2 baby gem lettuces, leaves separated

DRESSING
juice of 2 limes
1 tbsp fish sauce
1 tbsp caster sugar
1 tbsp rice vinegar

SERVES 4–6

SALAD
½ small green cabbage,
  finely shredded
½ small red cabbage,
  finely shredded
1 carrot, peeled and
  finely shredded
2 shallots, peeled and
  thinly sliced
2 Thai chillies, thinly
  sliced (deseeded, if
  you prefer)
1 celery stalk, thinly
  sliced
small handful of Thai
  basil
small handful of mint

DRESSING
juice of 1 grapefruit
juice of 2 limes
2 tbsp fish sauce
2 tbsp granulated sugar
1 tbsp vegetable oil

Sweet and sour cabbage salad

As much as I love cooked cabbage, it can be equally delicious raw – particularly here in this Vietnamese version of coleslaw. This recipe cannot be thrown together at the last minute, though, as it is vital that the salad sits in the dressing to allow the cabbage to soften and the flavours to develop and change. For an extra sour element I have added the juice of a grapefruit. This is best served as an accompaniment to other main dishes.

Place all the ingredients for the dressing in a bowl and whisk together until the sugar has dissolved. Ideally, prepare the dressing a few hours in advance so that the flavours can develop.

In a large serving bowl, mix together all the salad ingredients. Pour the dressing on top and allow to sit for up to 1 hour before serving.

Crispy pig's ear salad

The Vietnamese are advocates of nose-to-tail eating, so in this book I had to include at least one recipe that featured a less-common cut of meat. I served this pig's ear salad as the second out of seven pork courses on my final evening in Hanoi, and it was well received. My Vietnamese sous chefs were raving about how much they loved pig's ear and couldn't stop nibbling away. They like to eat the ears simply boiled, but I prefer them pan-fried and crispy. Give them a try if you are feeling adventurous.

Bring a pan of salted water to the boil. Add the sugar and vinegar and gently simmer the pigs' ears for 1 hour. Remove and allow to cool. Once cool, finely slice into thin strips. Dust the slices in plain flour and shake off the excess. Heat the oil in a frying pan and sauté the ears for 3–4 minutes until crisp and golden.

Mix together the carrot, shallots, chilli, papaya and fresh herbs in a large bowl.

To make the dressing, whisk together all the ingredients in a bowl to combine.

Pour the dressing over the salad and toss well to coat. Arrange on serving plates and place the crispy pig's ear on top. Serve scattered with roasted peanuts and crispy shallots.

SERVES 4

PIG'S EAR
2 tbsp sugar
2 tbsp white wine
  vinegar
2 pigs' ears
plain flour, for dusting
2 tbsp vegetable oil

SALAD
1 carrot, peeled and
  julienned
2 shallots, peeled and
  thinly sliced
1 red chilli, thinly sliced
1 small green papaya,
  peeled and sliced
handful of fresh herbs,
  including mint, basil
  and coriander, torn

DRESSING
1 tbsp caster sugar
1 tbsp fish sauce
juice of 1 lime
1 tbsp rice vinegar
1 garlic clove, peeled
  and finely chopped
1 tsp minced ginger
½ red chilli, finely diced

GARNISH
2 tbsp roasted peanuts,
  crushed
2 tbsp crispy shallots
  (page 266)

SERVES 4

SALAD
2 medium English
cucumbers, peeled
and cored
1 tbsp salt
1–2 tbsp granulated
sugar
1 red pepper, thinly
sliced
100g beansprouts

DRESSING
6 tbsp rice vinegar
3 tbsp granulated sugar
2 tbsp water
handful of mint leaves,
shredded
1 garlic clove, peeled
and finely diced
1 tbsp minced ginger
1 red chilli, thinly sliced
2 shallots, peeled and
thinly sliced
pinch of salt

Marinated cucumber salad

This popular Vietnamese salad, *Nom dua chuot*, is pure simplicity. I love cucumbers as they are very refreshing and also amazingly versatile because they absorb so much flavour. The cucumbers pickle and their flesh softens with the rice vinegar and sugar, but the addition of peppers and beansprouts gives the salad texture and crunch. I have finished the salad with a fragrant dressing made with ginger, garlic, chilli and mint.

This light salad is perfect in the summer months when the weather gets hot. It was just what I needed in Hanoi where the temperature gauge was pushing 40 degrees.

Slice the cucumbers diagonally and place them in a colander. Sprinkle with some salt and sugar and leave to sit for 15 minutes to allow any excess moisture to drain away. Rinse with cold water and then, in batches, place the pieces in a cloth and wring out any excess moisture, taking care not tear the cucumbers.

Mix together all the dressing ingredients, whisking in the sugar until it dissolves.

To construct the salad, place the cucumber, pepper and beansprouts in a dish and pour over the dressing. Toss well, then allow the salad to sit for around 10–15 minutes before serving, so that the cucumber is marinated.

Glass noodle crab salad

The Thai name of this salad, *Yum woon sen*, derives from the type of noodles used in it. Locally they are known as *Woon sen*, but in the Western world they are called glass noodles, because when cooked they become transparent.

There are endless ways to prepare glass-noodle salads, but I loved this version, which I sampled for lunch one day in Chiang Mai, because the noodles and crab combination reminded me of one of my favourite pasta dishes. Gently frying the crab with chilli and garlic infuses the meat flakes with their flavours, and the thin noodles make this a delicate dish. When buying crab meat, get the freshest available and, to be on the safe side, pick through the meat and discard any hidden shell before cooking.

Prepare the noodles by placing them in warm water for 6–7 minutes until softened, or follow the packet instructions. Drain well and cut the noodles into 10cm strips with a pair of scissors. Prepare the crab meat by picking through the meat, checking for any loose pieces of shell.

Place a wok or frying pan over a medium heat and heat the oil. Sauté the chillies, garlic and spring onions for 1–2 minutes and season with salt and pepper. Add the crab meat, stir together and allow to heat through.

In a mixing bowl, mix the noodles, the cooked crab and all the remaining salad ingredients except for the mint leaves.

Mix all the dressing ingredients together and whisk until the honey dissolves. Taste for seasoning and add more lime, sugar or fish sauce as desired and toss into the salad.

Divide the salad amongst four plates and serve immediately, garnished with mint leaves.

SERVES 4–6

SALAD

200g dried glass or
 mung bean noodles
400g white crab meat
2 tbsp vegetable oil
1 red bird's eye chilli,
 deseeded and thinly
 sliced
1 green bird's eye chilli,
 deseeded and thinly
 sliced
2 garlic cloves, peeled
 and finely chopped
2 spring onions, sliced
sea salt and freshly
 ground black pepper
10 cherry tomatoes,
 halved
1 red pepper, thinly
 sliced
small handful of
 coriander, shredded
small handful of
 Chinese celery leaves,
 shredded
small handful of mint,
 shredded, to garnish

DRESSING

1 garlic clove, peeled
 and thinly sliced
juice of 3 limes
3 tbsp fish sauce
4 tsp honey

Soups

Rice soup with marinated salmon and ginger

Fresh asparagus and crab soup

Pork-bone tea broth

Stuffed cucumber soup

Hot and sour prawn soup

Beef pho

Chicken, coconut and galangal soup

Curry laksa

Prawn and pork broth with rice noodles

Rice soup with marinated salmon and ginger

Also known as rice congee or *chao*, this rice soup is a staple of the Vietnamese diet, often served to those suffering from a cold or ailment. It can be produced with much simplicity, the rice just needs cooking slowly in the broth so the starches are released and the soup takes on a porridge-like consistency. For this *chao* the salmon is cured in the marinade, then spooned into the bottom of the bowl and the hot porridge ladled on top. As the soup is mixed together, the salmon gently 'cooks'.

This dish was inspired by a little hole in the wall in Hanoi, where the rice porridge was topped with a poached egg. It really brings the dish together; when the oozing yellow yolk is broken into the rice, the *chao* becomes even richer. It may not look like the most appetising of soups, but it is truly delicious.

Soak the jasmine rice in some water and move the grains around to release the starch. Drain off the starchy water and repeat this process two or three times. In a large saucepan, place the rice, chicken stock, galangal, spring onion and lime leaves. Bring the mixture to a very gentle simmer, not to a boil, then partially cover the rice and cook for about 1 hour or until you achieve a glutinous texture and a porridge-like consistency. After 1 hour the soup should be thick, creamy and white and there should be little separation between the rice and liquid.

To prepare the salmon, cut the fish into small chunks and place the remaining fish ingredients in the same bowl. Mix together to coat the salmon and allow the fish to marinate while the rice is simmering.

Place the salmon chunks in the bottom of individual soup bowls, carefully ladle the soup over and arrange a poached egg on top. Garnish with the dill, spring onions, coriander and crispy shallots. Finish with a grinding of white pepper and serve immediately.

SERVES 4–6

RICE SOUP
125g jasmine rice
1.5 litres chicken stock
2cm knob of galangal, peeled and bashed
1 spring onion, cut in half lengthways
2 kaffir lime leaves

FISH
400g salmon fillets, skinless
2cm knob of ginger, peeled and julienned
juice of 2 limes
2 tbsp fish sauce
2 tbsp light soy sauce
1 chilli, deseeded and finely sliced

GARNISH
4 poached eggs
small handful of dill sprigs
4 spring onions, finely shredded
small handful of coriander leaves
4 tbsp crispy shallots (see page 266)
freshly ground white pepper

Fresh asparagus and crab soup

SERVES 4

2 bunches thin green
asparagus (about 400g
or 24 spears)

2 litres chicken stock

2 tsp fish sauce

sea salt and freshly
ground black pepper

2 tbsp vegetable oil

1 chilli, deseeded (if
you prefer) and
finely diced

1 garlic clove, peeled
and minced

1 tsp minced ginger

2 shallots, peeled and
finely diced

300g white crab meat,
picked

2 eggs, beaten

2 spring onions, sliced,
to garnish

small handful coriander
leaves, to garnish

I am a big fan of asparagus, and when it comes into season my head goes into overdrive with recipes. So you can imagine my excitement when I saw this soup in Mui Ne. If I could read Vietnamese, the name of the soup, *Sup mang tay cua*, would have given me a clue to what was in it, as '*mang tay*' can be literally translated as asparagus or Western bamboo.

It was the French who first imported asparagus into Vietnam, as an expensive luxury ingredient, so this soup would only have been prepared for special occasions. However, times have changed. For the best flavour, use both the freshest crab and asparagus – it will make a huge difference to the sweetness of the soup.

Cut the asparagus spears in half, reserving the tips for use in the soup and the stalks for the base. Bring the stock to the boil and add the fish sauce, a pinch of pepper and asparagus tips and cook for 1 minute. Remove with a slotted spoon and refresh in cold water, then set aside. Add the asparagus stalks to the broth (these won't be served but will add their flavour to the liquid) and simmer for 20 minutes.

To prepare the crab, place a wok or small frying pan over a medium heat and heat the vegetable oil. Sauté the chilli, garlic, ginger and shallots for 1–2 minutes and season with salt and pepper. Add the crab meat, stir together and allow to heat through.

After 20 minutes, remove the asparagus stems from the broth and discard. Turn up the heat so that the water is boiling and whisk to form a swirl in the pan. Gradually add in the beaten eggs, reduce the heat and allow the eggs to form thin strands as they cook.

Add the blanched asparagus tips and warm through for 1–2 minutes or until cooked through. Neatly divide the cooked crab mixture between four bowls and spoon over the asparagus soup. Garnish with spring onions and coriander leaves to serve.

Pork-bone tea broth

This herbal soup, *Bak kut the*, is originally Chinese but is popular in Malaysia. It is made by braising spare ribs in a mixture of spices and a thick soy-sauce broth until the meat is tender and falling off the bone. Although it is usually served at breakfast, I think it would make a great hearty soup for lunch or dinner. It could even be considered a stew, because of the way in which the meat is braised.

Traditionally the broth is simmered with a selection of Chinese herbs, including angelica, lovage roots, liquorice and other lesser-known herbs. These are readily available, combined, in specialist Chinese supermarkets and online, but if you can't get hold of these herbs, just leave them out. This soup is often served in a clay pot, which many believe enhances the flavour.

Strain the dried mushrooms through a sieve, catching the soaking liquid in a bowl and setting aside the mushrooms for later. Place a large stockpot or clay pot over a medium heat and add the chicken stock, shiitake soaking liquid, *bak kut the* packet, spices, garlic and peppercorns. Reduce the heat to low and simmer for 30 minutes.

Meanwhile, place the pork ribs in a separate saucepan, cover with cold water and bring to the boil for 5 minutes, removing any scum that floats to the top. Drain.

After the broth has been infusing for 30 minutes, add the pork ribs to the pan along with the soy and oyster sauces. With the lid on, simmer very gently for 1–1½ hours until the meat is tender. If the meat looks like it is shrinking and about to fall off the bone, remove it from the broth and set it aside. Remove the spice bag.

Strain the broth through a colander or sieve and return the liquid to the stockpot or clay pot. Reduce it, if need be, and return the meat to the soup with the rehydrated shiitake and fresh mushrooms. Heat gently for 3–4 minutes. Check for seasoning, ladle the soup into bowls and garnish with chopped coriander.

SERVES 4

15g dried shiitake
  mushrooms, soaked
  in approx. 200ml
  hot water
2 litres chicken stock
1 packet *bak kut the*
  spices
5 star anise
1 cinnamon stick
½ tsp fennel seeds
4 cloves
1 garlic bulb, split
  in half
1 tsp black peppercorns
1kg pork spare ribs, cut
  into 7.5cm pieces
3 tbsp dark sweet
  soy sauce
3 tbsp light soy sauce
1 tbsp oyster sauce
100g fresh mushrooms
  (oyster, shiitake, etc.),
  sliced
small handful of
  chopped coriander
  leaves, to garnish

Stuffed cucumber soup

SERVES 4

KROEUNG PASTE

2 garlic cloves, peeled
   and roughly chopped
1 chilli, finely chopped
3 shallots, peeled and
   roughly chopped
2cm knob of galangal,
   peeled and roughly
   chopped
4 kaffir lime leaves
2cm knob of turmeric
   root, peeled
sea salt and white
   pepper
vegetable oil, for frying

SOUP

125g pork mince
1 large cucumber,
   peeled
1 litre chicken stock
3 tbsp palm sugar
3 tbsp fish sauce
2 spring onions, finely
   sliced
small handful of
   coriander, chopped
small handful of holy
   basil, roughly chopped

I first saw this soup in Phnom Penh, in Cambodia, at the Central Market. This famous Art-Deco building is a city landmark and houses every meat, fish, fruit and vegetable imaginable. Amongst them were rows of bitter gourds, a vegetable that looks like a cucumber with a knobbly skin. I had tried them years ago and wasn't a huge fan, but I was curious to see if Cambodia could change my mind. As I was leaving the market I spotted a little street restaurant ladling out bitter-gourd slices stuffed with pork mince that had been poached in a light chicken broth. They looked delicate and pretty and, despite the scorching humidity it looked appetising – so I gave it a try.

While I loved the idea of the soup, I still didn't like the bitter gourd, so I have recreated it using cucumber. It is a light dish, which would suit the health-conscious and also makes it perfect for serving in the summer months or as a starter.

To prepare the kroeung paste, place all the ingredients, except the oil, in a blender and pulse until smooth. Heat 1 tablespoon of oil in a pan and fry the paste for 2–3 minutes to release the flavours. Remove from the heat and allow to cool.

Add the kroeung paste to the pork mince, mix well and season. Remove both ends of the cucumber, cut it into 1.5cm slices and with a spoon scoop out the seeds. Fill the hole with the ground pork and secure with two toothpicks inserted crosswise through each piece. Do not overstuff, or the filling will fall out during poaching.

Place a large saucepan over a medium heat and, stirring, add the stock, palm sugar and fish sauce. Gently place the stuffed cucumber slices in the broth and cook for 15–20 minutes, partially covered with a lid, until the cucumber is softened and the meat is cooked – the stuffing will become firm.

Carefully remove the toothpicks and ladle the cucumber slices into bowls. Garnish with spring onions, chopped coriander and holy basil.

Hot and sour prawn soup

On my last day in Thailand we stopped for lunch in a heaving café on the way to Bang Luang, north of Bangkok. In the outside kitchen one woman manned two woks with ease, cooking at the speed of light, and inside were a few rice steamers and two chefs grafting away over small gas burners. While sitting on the obligatory green garden chairs around a plastic-covered table, a selection of dishes was served, including the best bowl of hot and sour soup I tasted during my travels round Thailand.

This recipe is inspired by that soup – *Tom yam goong nam khon;* in my version the lime and tamarind juice provide the sour element and the chillies the heat. If you leave the prawn shells in they will give the broth its characteristic red colour.

To prepare the tom yam paste, place a wok over a medium heat and add the oil. When hot, add the remaining ingredients and fry for 2–3 minutes, until the paste has turned golden brown. Remove from the heat and set aside.

Peel and de-vein the prawns (reserving the heads and shells) leaving the tails intact. Place the prawns in a bowl and refrigerate until needed. Heat the oil in a large pan, add the reserved prawn shells and heads and cook for 10 minutes over a moderately high heat, tossing frequently, until they are a deep orange colour. Add the garlic, chilli, shallots and galangal and cook for around 2 minutes, to infuse their flavours. Add 500ml of stock and bring to the boil. Add the tom yam paste and mix well. Add the remaining stock along with the lemongrass, turmeric and four lime leaves. Simmer for 20 minutes. Red scum will form on the top of the liquid, but do not remove this.

Strain the broth, discarding the heads and shells, and return to the pan. Add the fish sauce, lime juice, sugar and remaining lime leaves, stirring to combine. Heat gently for 2–3 minutes. Add the prawns, mushrooms and tomatoes and cook for 3–4 minutes until the prawns have turned bright pink and are cooked through. About 1 minute before serving, mix in the squid and poach until cooked through.

Serve in warmed soup bowls, garnished with spring onion and herbs.

SERVES 4

TOM YAM PASTE
2 tbsp vegetable oil
5–6 tbsp red Thai curry paste
3 tbsp fish sauce
50g dried prawns
3 tbsp palm sugar
1 tsp salt

SOUP
500g whole tiger prawns
4 tbsp olive oil
4 garlic cloves, peeled and crushed
1 chilli, deseeded and sliced
2 shallots, peeled and roughly chopped
2.5cm knob of galangal, peeled and bashed
2.5 litres fish stock
3 lemongrass stalks, trimmed and bashed
1 turmeric root, peeled
9 kaffir lime leaves, shredded
1 tbsp fish sauce
juice of 1–2 limes
1 tbsp palm sugar
100g enoki mushrooms
14 cherry tomatoes, cut in half
200g squid, cleaned and cut into rings
thinly sliced spring onion and handful of coriander leaves and shredded sweet basil, to garnish

Beef pho

SERVES 4

BROTH

2kg oxtail, jointed and
  cut into pieces
3 onions, peeled and
  quartered
7.5cm knob of ginger,
  skin on and roughly
  chopped
3 carrots, peeled and
  roughly chopped
2 celery stalks, roughly
  chopped
2 tbsp vegetable oil
6 star anise
6 cloves
7.5cm cinnamon stick
1 tsp fennel seeds
1 tsp black peppercorns
2 kaffir lime leaves
1 lemongrass stalk,
  trimmed and bruised
3 bay leaves
3 tbsp fish sauce, plus
  extra to serve
  (optional)
3 tbsp palm sugar, plus
  extra to serve
  (optional)

This rich and flavoursome dish is replicated across the globe; I met people who will travel great distances for a good bowl of Pho, although in Hanoi locals argued that the best version could be eaten there.

Pho was originally a breakfast or snack food but it has become so popular that it is now eaten throughout the day. It is simply a fragrant broth that is poured over the 'Pho' – thick rice noodles and thinly sliced beef – then garnished with the freshest herbs. Some soups can be made in minutes, but this broth is not something that can be rushed. To achieve the deep beef flavour, I would recommend making it from scratch. It is also best to make the beef broth a day in advance so it can cool and the fat can separate and be skimmed off before reheating, to prevent the broth becoming oily.

In Vietnam they serve this alongside a platter of garnishes. I think this is a really great idea and it allows you or your guests to pick and choose your favourite ingredients to add to the soup.

To prepare the broth, preheat the oven to 220°C/Fan 200°C/Gas 7. Spread out the oxtail bones in a large roasting tin with the onions, ginger, carrots and celery. Drizzle with a little vegetable oil to coat. Roast for between 45 minutes–1 hour, turning the bones over halfway, until evenly browned. Be careful not to let the onions and ginger burn, you just want them browned. When they are ready, remove from the oven. Pick through the onion and ginger, discarding any burnt bits if necessary.

Now place a large stockpot over a medium heat. Toss in all the spices and the peppercorns and dry roast for 1–2 minutes until fragrant. Add in the roasted oxtail bones and vegetables and mix well. Pour in 4.5 litres of water or enough so that the bones are fully submerged.

Add the lime leaves, lemongrass, bay leaves, fish sauce and palm sugar and mix well. Simmer the stock with the lid on for 2–3 hours, occasionally using a spoon to skim off any excess grease and oils.

When the broth is ready, let it stand for a few minutes before gently passing through a fine sieve or cheesecloth. Shred the oxtail meat off

the bones. This meat can be served with the soup. There will be excess meat, so save some for another dish. Discard everything else.

Leave the beef broth to cool, preferably overnight in the fridge, allowing the fat to separate and rise to the top. Once the fat has settled on top and cooled, remove it and discard.

To finish the soup, cover the beef in cling film and place it in the freezer. This will firm up the beef and make it easier to slice. After 30 minutes, remove the beef from the freezer, unwrap it and thinly slice it against the grain. Cut into thin strips.

Meanwhile, soak the rice noodles in hot water for 20 minutes or according to the packet instructions. Drain, then cook for 1 minute in lightly salted boiling water. Drain again. Don't let the noodles overcook, you still want them to be slightly firm.

On a plate or platter, carefully arrange the spring onions, chilli, Thai basil, coriander, beansprouts, lime wedges and chive flowers (if using).

When you are ready to serve, reheat the broth and bring to a boil. Taste and add more fish sauce or palm sugar if necessary. Place a heap of noodles in large soup bowls and carefully place slices of the raw beef as well as the oxtail meat, if using, on top.

Carefully ladle the boiling broth into the bowls, making sure all the beef is covered. Serve immediately alongside the platter of garnishes.

TO SERVE
150g beef sirloin or fillet
150–200g small flat rice noodles
4 spring onions, finely sliced
1 small red chilli, thinly sliced
small handful of Thai basil leaves
small handful of coriander leaves
100g beansprouts
2 limes, halved
small handful of chive flowers (optional)

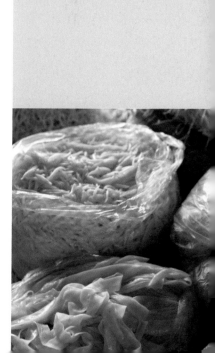

SERVES 4

200ml chicken stock

400ml coconut milk

320ml coconut cream

6 kaffir lime leaves,
  shredded

2 shallots, peeled and
  thinly sliced

2 lemongrass stalks,
  trimmed and bruised

5cm knob of galangal,
  peeled and
  thinly sliced

4 tbsp fish sauce

juice of 2 limes

1 tbsp palm sugar

1 red Thai chilli, cut in
  half lengthways

3 skinless chicken
  breasts, thinly sliced

100g oyster
  mushrooms, thinly
  sliced (optional)

GARNISH

small handful of
  coriander leaves

sliced spring onions

2 Thai red chillies,
  finely sliced (optional)

Chicken, coconut and galangal soup

This *Tom kha gai* is the ultimate comfort soup; it is a bit like a Thai version of classic chicken soup, except with a smooth, rich, coconut broth.

Both coconut milk and coconut cream are used in this recipe – using only cream would be too rich and using only milk would dilute the flavour. The success of this soup is dependent on infusing the lemongrass, lime leaves, galangal and chilli in the coconut cream, milk and chicken stock. The longer you infuse, the stronger the flavour. However, the main flavour in this dish comes from the galangal (the *Kha* in the title); although galangal and ginger are members of the same family, their taste is very different, with galangal having a woody, slightly peppery taste.

Place a stockpot over a medium heat and pour in the chicken stock, coconut milk and cream. Add the lime leaves, shallots, lemongrass, galangal, fish sauce, lime juice, palm sugar and chilli. Simmer the soup base for around 15–20 minutes or longer, until the flavour has developed.

Strain the soup and, using the back of a ladle, squeeze out as much liquid and flavour back into the strained soup as possible. Place the flavoured soup base back over a medium heat and add the chicken and mushrooms and simmer for around 4–5 minutes until the chicken is cooked.

When you are ready to serve, ladle the soup into warmed bowls and garnish with the coriander leaves, spring onions and chillies, if using.

Curry laksa

I found myself devouring this soup late one night after finishing work in Kuala Lumpur. A big bowl of yellow mee noodles were sitting in a sweet, coconut, fishy broth, topped with the widest variety of fresh ingredients, including cucumber, mint leaves and beansprouts.

For that extra kick, this dish should be served with sambal chilli paste, and you definitely need chopsticks to help you slurp up the noodles and pick up every last bit. Well, that's what I did!

To prepare the laksa paste, place all the ingredients in a blender with a little water and blend until smooth.

Peel the tiger prawns, reserving the heads and shells. Place a medium-sized saucepan over a high heat with 4 tablespoons of oil, then add the prawn heads and shells and fry for around 5–10 minutes until they are bright red in colour. Remove the heads and shells from the pan. Add 2 tablespoons more oil to the pan and fry the spice paste until it becomes fragrant and starts turning a golden brown. Add the fish stock and simmer for 10–12 minutes, to let the flavours infuse.

Add the coconut milk, lime juice and fish sauce and stir well, then cook for a further 5–10 minutes. Add the prawns to the soup and allow them to poach for 3–4 minutes, until cooked through. Stir in the tofu puffs and warm through.

Meanwhile, prepare some of the toppings. Poach the chicken in a little chicken stock or water with the lime leaves and galangal for 12–14 minutes. Peel, deseed and julienne the cucumber and finely slice the chillies and red onion.

To serve, place the cooked noodles (reheat or warm them before serving) in warmed soup bowls and ladle the laksa on top. Garnish by arranging all the topping ingredients in sections on top and serve immediately.

SERVES 4

LAKSA PASTE
8 shallots, peeled and roughly chopped
2.5cm knob of ginger, peeled and chopped
2 lemongrass stalks, white part only, sliced
2 garlic cloves, peeled
2cm knob of turmeric root, peeled and chopped
2–4 tbsp sambal chilli paste or 2 dried red chillies, rehydrated
1 tsp shrimp paste

SOUP
500g tiger prawns, shell on
vegetable oil, for cooking
1 litre fish stock
400ml coconut milk
juice of 1 lime
1 tsp fish sauce
60g tofu puffs
425g fresh cooked thick egg noodles (*mee*)

TOPPINGS
2 chicken breasts
chicken stock or water
2 kaffir lime leaves
4 slices of galangal, peeled
¼ cucumber
2 red chillies
½ red onion, peeled
4 tbsp crispy shallots (see page 266)
handful of beansprouts
handful of mint leaves
1 lime, cut into 4 wedges

Prawn and pork broth with rice noodles

At 6 o'clock one morning I found myself sitting on a little wooden boat being bossed around by an amazing local woman, called Mrs Diep, as we paddled upstream along the Mekong Delta to the famous Can Tho floating market. It was an unforgettable sight; large boats were stacked full of ingredients which they were selling to passing boats that just about stopped in time to catch the watermelons, jackfruits or other offerings.

For 37 years Mrs Diep has prepared her *Hu tieu* broth every day without fail, to sell to the people on these boats. She sells around 80 bowls daily, but when she was younger and stronger the market was not so tough and she could sell up to 150 bowls a day. Luckily, her income (around $20 a day) is still enough to support her 15 grandchildren. The popularity of Mrs Diep's *Hu tieu*, with its balance of sweetness in the broth, has made her somewhat legendary in the area.

A good *Hu tieu* broth should be clear. To achieve this you need to boil the pork bones and dried prawns at the lowest heat for as long as possible – the broth should never produce a bubble. Top it with a fresh herbed salad, kumquat or limes and any additional garnishes such as coriander or carrot and some fish sauce. This is also traditionally served with sliced liver, but you can omit this if you prefer.

Place the pork bones in a large stockpot, cover with cold water and bring to the boil. Blanch the pork bones to remove any scum – this should take around 10 minutes. Drain the water and impurities and add the garlic, ginger, onions, carrots and daikon radish to the pork and cover again with water.

Place the dried prawns in a food processor or pestle and mortar and pound until fine. Add to the pork broth and simmer for as long as you possibly can – ideally 3–6 hours – at a very low heat. (Don't have the heat too high otherwise the stock will turn cloudy.)

Strain the stock through a muslin cloth (or tea towel) into a clean pan. Add the sugar and fish sauce to taste.

Poach the pork strips in the broth for 6–8 minutes until cooked. Remove, drain and set aside. If you are adding liver, heat the vegetable oil in a frying pan. Season the liver with salt and pepper and fry for 1–2 minutes on each side. Remove and set aside.

When you are ready to serve, blanch the noodles in hot water until softened and then drain. Divide amongst four bowls and ladle the broth on top.

Garnish with the pork, liver (if using), beansprouts, spring onions, herbs, crispy shallots, bamboo shoots and kumquat or lime halves to serve.

Tip: If you have broth left over you can freeze it and use it as a base for other dishes, or for the next time you want to eat this.

SERVES 4

PORK BROTH
2kg pork bones, washed
½ bulb of garlic
10cm knob of ginger, peeled and bashed
2 red onions, peeled and cut into quarters
3 carrots, peeled and roughly chopped
1 daikon radish, peeled and roughly chopped
50g dried prawns
1 tbsp caster sugar, to taste
3 tbsp fish sauce, to taste

TO SERVE
250g pork loin, sinew removed, thinly sliced
1 tbsp vegetable oil
150g pork liver, finely sliced (optional)
sea salt and freshly ground black pepper
150g rice noodles
small handful of beansprouts
2 spring onions, finely sliced
small handful of coriander leaves and basil, chopped
small handful of crispy shallots (see page 266)
small handful of bamboo shoots (optional)
2 kumquats or limes, halved

Stir-fries

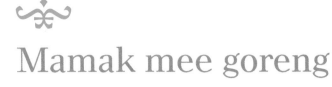

Mamak mee goreng

SERVES 4

SAUCE

2 tbsp chilli sauce

2 tbsp oyster sauce

1 tbsp tomato ketchup

2 tbsp dark sweet
  soy sauce

2 tbsp peanut oil

STIR-FRY

2 tbsp peanut oil

2 garlic cloves, peeled
  and finely chopped

2 shallots, peeled and
  finely sliced

2 chicken breasts,
  skinless and boneless,
  finely sliced

1 potato, peeled, boiled
  and diced

2 tsp curry powder

50g beansprouts

500g fresh cooked
  yellow noodles (mee)

2 squid, cleaned and cut
  into rings

GARNISH

2 spring onions, finely
  sliced

8 large poached prawns,
  peeled and de-veined

2 red chillies, finely
  sliced

1 lime, cut into wedges

2 eggs, hard-boiled and
  quartered lengthways

There are hundreds of *mamak* stalls all over Kuala Lumpur, frying up this and many other dishes. Literally translated, *mamak* means uncle, but it actually refers to the Muslim immigrants who have settled in Malaysia.

A popular *mamak* stall can attract hundreds of people sitting out, eating, relaxing and washing down their food with *Teh tarik* – pulled tea (see page 257). Unlike in Pad Thai or *Char keow tuay*, in this recipe the noodles should be the *mee* yellow noodles, which are stir-fried with potatoes, chicken and tomato-based, spicy curry sauce. The finished dish is then served with an array of garnishes, including boiled egg and poached prawns.

To prepare the sauce, combine all the ingredients in a bowl, mix well and set aside.

Heat the peanut oil in a wok and cook the garlic and shallots for 1 minute. Toss in the chicken, potato and curry powder and stir-fry for 3–4 minutes until the chicken and potato have coloured, and the potato is crispy.

Add the sauce to the pan and mix well, ensuring that all the ingredients are evenly coated. Allow the sauce to boil and reduce slightly. Add the beansprouts and noodles and stir-fry for a further 3–4 minutes, until the noodles start to crisp up in some places, then remove. The wok should now be quite dry. When the noodles are ready, toss in the squid and continue to cook for a further 1–2 minutes until it is ready.

Divide between four plates and garnish each with the spring onions, poached prawns, red chillies, lime wedges and egg quarters.

Pineapple-fried rice with chicken and cashew nuts

It's not often that you see pineapple bushes growing along the side of the road, but this was a common sight in Southern Thailand. The hot climate makes Thailand one of the largest pineapple growers in the world, and I knew it wouldn't be long before I would see the sticky, yellow, sweet flesh being thrown around a wok.

One of the most common and easily prepared pineapple dishes is this *Kao pad sapparot*, which translates as fried rice with pineapple. I really enjoyed the version I ate in Ao Nang, where chicken and cashew nuts were also added to the stir-fry. In this recipe I have included red pepper for some extra colour and crunch. Traditionally the pineapple flesh is scooped out so the shell can be used to serve the rice in, but I prefer to simply spoon it into bowls and eat it while still steaming. This is a dish you will want to eat over and over again.

Heat a wok until very hot, then add the vegetable oil. Add the chopped garlic, ginger and chillies and stir-fry for 30 seconds. Cut the chicken into bite-sized pieces and toss into the wok and cook for 2–3 minutes until the chicken changes colour and the edges turn brown. Toss in the roasted cashew nuts, curry powder, turmeric and cinnamon and stir-fry until fragrant. Toss in the sliced pepper, pineapple and spring onions. Stir-fry for 30 seconds before adding the fish sauce, soy sauce and sugar.

Add in the rice and mix well for 3–4 minutes. Remove from the wok, divide equally among four plates, garnish with coriander and serve immediately.

SERVES 4

3 tbsp vegetable oil
1 garlic clove, peeled and finely chopped
1 tbsp finely chopped ginger
2 red chillies, deseeded and finely diced
2 large boneless, skinless chicken breasts
50g cashew nuts, roasted
1 tbsp curry powder
2 tsp ground turmeric
1 tsp ground cinnamon
1 red pepper, thinly sliced
1 small pineapple, peeled, cored and diced
4 spring onions, finely sliced
1 tbsp fish sauce
2 tbsp light soy sauce
1 tbsp caster sugar
300g cooked long grain rice
handful of coriander, chopped, to garnish

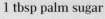

SERVES 4

2 tbsp vegetable oil

5 small shallots, finely
sliced

1 red chilli, deseeded
(optional) and sliced

1 tbsp Thai red curry
paste

500g raw medium
prawns, peeled and
de-veined

100g stink beans or
broad beans, podded
and sliced in half

1–2 tbsp tamarind paste

1 tbsp palm sugar

Prawn and stink bean stir-fry

Once you have tried a stink bean (known in Thailand as *sator*) you won't ever forget the taste. For me that moment came at a family dinner in Southern Thailand where one of the dishes on offer was this. As I went to eat the stink bean I could sense about twelve eyes on me, awaiting my reaction. I chewed and swallowed it; the taste was bitter and lingering, the smell unusual – almost gassy. I must have had a pained expression while chewing as this prompted the children and parents to start laughing. It is great when food can create a reaction, whether you like it or not – which for me was the latter.

The Thais are very fond of this bean, and I imagine if it is a taste you have grown up with you become accustomed to it. Overall the stir-fry was delicious, though, so I decided to make it with earthy broad beans instead of stink beans.

Heat a wok until very hot, add the oil and fry the shallots and chilli for 2–3 minutes to soften. Add the Thai red curry paste and cook for 1–2 minutes until it turns golden brown, then add the prawns and continue cooking.

Add the stink or broad beans and stir-fry for 2–3 minutes so that the prawns and beans cook through. Finally, add the tamarind paste and palm sugar. Add a splash more water to loosen the stir-fry, allow the liquid to reduce for around 1 minute, then serve immediately.

Char kway teow

This is a really cheap and popular dish in Malaysia. Traditionally the noodles and seafood are stir-fried in lard, but for a healthier and by no means less delicious version, I cook mine in oil.

In Kuala Lumpur, next to the stall where I was eating bull's penis (it's a Malay speciality, honestly!) stood a little hawker's stall dishing out *Char kway teow*. Our guide, H, told me that this dish should be served with blood cockles and other variations – including fish cakes or Chinese sausage. I tried a simpler version one lunchtime, which inspired this recipe: soft rice noodles and vegetables stir-fried with calamari, clams and prawns. The plate was empty before I knew it, but I still wanted more!

Soak the rice noodles in warm water for about 10 minutes until flexible and pliable, but not overly soft, or cook according to the packet instructions (some dried noodles need to be blanched in boiling water for several minutes to soften them).

In a bowl, mix together the soy sauces, fish sauce and 1 tablespoon of water.

Heat the oil in a wok or a large non-stick frying pan until hot. Add the crushed garlic and chilli paste and stir over a medium heat until fragrant. Add the Chinese sausage and pepper and stir-fry for 1–2 minutes. Add the clams with a splash of water and cover with a lid. Cook for 1–2 minutes then remove the lid and add the prawns and cabbage and cook for few minutes until the prawns are pink. Stir in the squid. Add the sauce, followed by the noodles.

Push the ingredients to the edges of the wok, forming a well in the centre. Add the rest of the oil and heat it. Add the beaten eggs and fry them together with the noodles.

Taste to see if the seasoning is to your liking. If not, add a bit more fish sauce and dark soy sauce. Add the beansprouts and spring onions and season to taste with pepper. Serve immediately.

SERVES 4

225g flat rice noodles
3 tbsp dark sweet
  soy sauce
1 tbsp dark soy sauce
1 tsp fish sauce
2 tbsp groundnut oil
3 garlic cloves, peeled
  and crushed
2 tbsp chilli paste
1 Chinese sausage,
  diced
1 green (or red) pepper,
  sliced
200g clams, washed
250g raw prawns,
  peeled and de-veined
100g Chinese cabbage,
  finely shredded
250g squid, cleaned and
  cut into rings
2 eggs, beaten
50g beansprouts
2 spring onions, finely
  sliced
pinch of ground white
  pepper

SERVES 4–6

1 small broccoli head,
  cut into small florets
2 tbsp fish sauce
1 tbsp rice vinegar
1 tsp sugar
1 tbsp oyster sauce
1 tbsp water
2 tbsp vegetable oil
1 garlic clove, peeled
  and finely diced
2 shallots, peeled and
  finely sliced
½ red pepper, thinly
  sliced
½ yellow pepper, thinly
  sliced
1 carrot, peeled and
  thinly sliced
100g shiitake
  mushrooms, sliced
100g sugar snap peas
pinch of white pepper

GARNISH (OPTIONAL)

small handful of
  coriander leaves

Vietnamese stir-fried vegetables

Vegetables play an important part in Vietnamese cuisine; no meal is complete without a plate of salad or stir-fried vegetables. The Vietnamese eat seasonally and their humid climate lends itself to growing a wide selection of vegetables, such as cauliflowers, carrots and chilli peppers. They cook vegetables to perfection; nearly every meal I ate there was accompanied by vegetables that were vibrant in colour and cooked until *al dente*.

The vegetables I have included here are some of my favourites and are a suggestion only. Cook what you like to eat, and for the best flavour choose ingredients that are seasonally available.

Place a medium-sized saucepan filled with water over a medium heat and bring to the boil. Drop in the broccoli and blanch for 3 minutes or until tender. Remove with a slotted spoon and place in a bowl of iced water or under a cold running tap to stop the cooking process. Drain, then place on kitchen paper to remove the water.

In a bowl mix together the fish sauce, vinegar, sugar, oyster sauce and water.

Before starting the stir-fry, make sure all of the ingredients are prepared, as there will be no time during the cooking. Place a wok over a high heat and add the oil. Toss in the garlic and shallots and stir-fry for 20 seconds until fragrant. Toss in the red and yellow peppers and the carrot and stir-fry for 30 seconds before adding in the mushrooms and sugar snap peas. After 1 minute, toss in the blanched broccoli and stir-fry for another 30 seconds. Finally, pour in the sauce mixture that you prepared earlier, along with some pepper, keeping the vegetables moving continuously and making sure the vegetables are coated. Allow the sauce to reduce by half then remove from the wok.

If you wish, garnish with coriander leaves. Serve immediately.

Venison stir-fry with lemongrass and coconut milk

Vietnam is notorious for eating a wide variety of animals; it is and will always be part of their culture. Venison, as I discovered, is a real favourite; with its delicate gamey flavour and lean meat, it can hold its own in a wok against strong flavours such as chilli and lemongrass. Traditionally venison is served alongside a sweet sauce, however this dish includes coconut milk, which makes an unusual but surprisingly delicious combination.

Marinating venison will help to tenderise the meat. As venison is such a lean meat, you need to take care to not overcook it in the wok; if you quickly sear it and set it aside while the remaining ingredients are stir-fried, the meat will remain tender.

Cover the venison in cling film and place it in the freezer. This will firm up the meat and make it easier to slice. After 30 minutes, take it out of the freezer, remove the cling film and thinly slice the meat against the grain. Cut into thin strips and place in a bowl.

To prepare the marinade for the venison, pour approximately 6 tablespoons of peanut oil (enough to cover the venison) into a shallow dish and scatter over the thyme. Lightly crush the peppercorns on a board, using the back of a pan, or in a mortar and pestle, then add to the dish along with the crushed garlic clove and one of the sliced lemongrass stalks. Give everything a stir then add the venison. Season with salt and then toss everything together, making sure the venison is coated thoroughly. Allow the venison to marinate for up to 1 hour.

Place a wok over a high heat and drain the oil from the marinade, reserving 2 tablespoons and adding them to the wok. Toss in the venison and stir-fry for 2–3 minutes until nicely browned. Keep the meat moving, so that it doesn't stick. Strain into a colander and catch the juices in a bowl underneath.

Wipe the wok clean and add 2 tablespoons of peanut oil. Toss in the chopped garlic, the shallots, chilli and remaining sliced lemongrass stalk and stir-fry for 30 seconds. Toss in the red pepper and mushrooms and stir-fry until the mushrooms are browned and peppers slightly wilted.

Add the oyster sauce and coconut milk to the wok and mix well. Allow the mixture to boil and reduce for 30 seconds before adding the venison and juices and the crushed peanuts. Stir-fry for around 1 minute, until all the vegetables are evenly coated and the sauce is thick and creamy.

Remove from the wok and serve immediately, garnished with mint.

SERVES 4

2 venison fillets, approx. 250g each
8 tbsp peanut oil
2 tsp thyme leaves
1 tbsp black peppercorns
3 garlic cloves, peeled and 1 crushed, 2 finely chopped
2 lemongrass stalks, trimmed and finely sliced
pinch of sea salt
3 shallots, peeled and thinly sliced
1 red chilli, thinly sliced
1 red pepper, thinly sliced
100g oyster mushrooms, halved
1–2 tbsp oyster sauce
200ml coconut milk
50g crushed roasted peanuts
small handful of mint, roughly chopped, to garnish

Stir-fried water spinach with garlic, fish sauce and lime

SERVES 4

1lb water spinach, stems removed, or pak choi, shredded
2 tbsp vegetable oil
4 garlic cloves, peeled and finely chopped
1 tbsp fish sauce
1 tbsp oyster sauce
juice of 2 limes
½ tsp ground white pepper, to taste

Water spinach – or, as it is otherwise known, 'morning glory' – is widely cooked throughout Southeast Asia, especially in Vietnam. It used to be a staple of the Vietnamese diet for those with little money, but now it is commonly cooked, regardless of one's income. The Vietnamese have been cooking this simple recipe for years, eating morning glory as part of their daily vegetable intake.

Morning glory can be identified by its long hollow stem and large, thin, pointed leaves. It grows in waterways or wet soil which, I think, helps it develop its earthy flavour. Water spinach can be found in Asian supermarkets, but suitable substitutes include Tenderstem broccoli, pak choi or spinach. For the latter two ingredients, blanching prior to stir-frying is not required.

To prepare the water spinach, snap off the fibrous woody stalk. Just like asparagus, it should naturally snap. Cut the remaining water spinach in half. Place a pot of water over a high heat and bring to the boil. Blanch the water spinach for 1 minute and then place in iced water or under a cold running tap to stop the cooking process. Drain thoroughly in a colander.

Now place a wok over a high heat and pour in the vegetable oil, swirling it round the pan to ensure an even coating. Toss in the garlic and stir-fry for 20 seconds to fragrance the oil, but do not let it burn. Immediately toss in the water spinach and keep it moving round the wok. Add the fish sauce, oyster sauce, lime juice and white pepper and stir-fry until the greens are wilted and heated through.

Remove from the wok and place on a serving platter or divide amongst individual plates.

Chicken, asparagus and green bean stir-fry

Thailand really brought me back to basics, and I was endlessly told that stir-fries should always be quick and simple. So when challenged to cook against Chef McDang, one of Thailand's best-known chefs, I wanted to create a stir-fry that would both impress and reflect my new-found understanding of Thai cooking. No dish is without a name, and a local chef called this *Pad cha*. *Pad* means fried, and *cha* describes the noise as the ingredients hit the sizzling wok.

The delicious flavours of this dish come from all the fresh ingredients used, but it is also infused with the spicy and fragrant green peppercorns in the chilli paste (get fresh green peppercorns on the vine for the best flavour). The addition of the fried quails' eggs was a last-minute decision to add a dainty garnish; however, they were not easy to find and I had to seek out the one woman in the village who had 'pheasant eggs', as they are also known as in Thailand.

To prepare the chilli paste, grind together all the ingredients in a food processor to a smooth paste. Heat 2 tablespoons of oil in a wok, add the chilli paste and cook for a few minutes to release the flavour. Thinly slice the chicken and stir-fry for 3–4 minutes. Add the oyster, fish and soy sauces and continue to cook for a further 1–2 minutes.

Remove the chicken from the wok and set aside, reserving the juices in the wok. Toss in the asparagus, beans and baby corn and cook for 1 minute, coating them in the chilli paste, until done but still crunchy. Finally, add the water spinach or pak choi and cook for 1–2 minutes. Taste and add a little palm sugar; if the sauce is too sticky, add 100–150ml water and reduce. Turn off the heat and set aside.

Heat some oil in a large pan over a medium-high heat, carefully crack the eggs open and drop them in. Fry for 1–1½ minutes until the whites are opaque and firm but the yolks are still quite runny.

Serve the stir-fry on four plates, top each with a quail's egg and garnish with the shallots and chillies. Accompany with steamed rice.

SERVES 4

CHILLI PASTE
8 garlic cloves, peeled
4–6 Thai chillies, stems removed
2 tsp green peppercorns
1 tbsp vegetable oil

STIR-FRY
vegetable oil, for frying
3 boneless, skinless chicken breasts
2 tbsp oyster sauce
1 tbsp fish sauce
3 tbsp dark soy sauce
1 bunch of asparagus, cut into pieces
250g long or French beans, cut into 1cm pieces
250g baby sweetcorn, cut into 1cm pieces
150g water spinach or pak choi, shredded
a little palm sugar

GARNISH
4 quails' eggs
crispy shallots
2 Thai red chillies, thinly sliced

Stir-fried pork with holy basil

I spent my first night in Bangkok standing in the middle of a busy night-market on a stall with the owner, otherwise known as Mr Whiskers. (I still don't know his actual name!) For years he has been cooking the chicken-based *Pad kraphao kai* to order, but the night I joined him he cooked a pork version – *Pad kraphao moo*. This market fare is the Thais' equivalent of fast food – except it is healthy and tasty.

The dish is so simple, based on the star flavouring of *kra phao* holy basil with its sharp, mentholated aroma and taste. There are many different basil strains available, but do not confuse this with Thai basil, which has a different flavour.

Place the Thai chillies and garlic in a pestle and mortar and pound together well to make a paste (alternatively, blend in a mini food processor until smooth). Heat the oil in a wok or a large non-stick frying pan until hot. Add the garlic and chilli paste and cook for 20 seconds, until fragrant. Toss in the pork and stir-fry for 2–3 minutes, until the pork has changed colour and the texture is firmer. Toss in the carrot, sweetcorn and lime leaves and continue to stir-fry for a further 1–2 minutes.

Add in the fish sauce, soy sauce, oyster sauce, palm sugar and white pepper and continue to stir-fry for 1 minute, mixing well to ensure that the pork is coated. Add the chicken stock and continue to heat for a few minutes until the liquid is reduced.

Stir in the holy basil towards the end and spoon onto a bed of cooked rice to serve.

SERVES 4

4–6 Thai red chillies, finely chopped (deseeded, if you prefer)

6–8 garlic cloves, peeled and finely chopped

3 tbsp groundnut oil

400g pork tenderloin, cut into strips

1 large carrot, peeled and cut into thin strips

200g baby sweetcorn, cut in ½ lengthways

2 small kaffir lime leaves, shredded

2 tbsp fish sauce

2 tbsp light soy sauce

2 tbsp oyster sauce

1 tbsp palm sugar

pinch of ground white pepper

175ml chicken stock

large handful of holy basil leaves, torn

SERVES 4

200g thin dried rice
  noodles
1 tbsp caster sugar
2 tbsp fish sauce
2 tbsp tamarind paste
1 tbsp chilli sauce
2 tbsp vegetable oil
1 shallot, peeled and
  chopped
2 garlic cloves, peeled
  and sliced
1 red chilli, deseeded
  and sliced
250g beef, such as rump
  steak or sirloin, sliced
  thinly
2 medium eggs, beaten
100g beansprouts
2 spring onions,
  trimmed and green
  parts cut into finger
  lengths
juice of 1 lime
1 tbsp palm sugar
2 tbsp dark sweet
  soy sauce
2 tbsp light soy sauce

GARNISH

8 tbsp roasted chopped
  peanuts, to garnish
lime wedges, to garnish

Beef pad Thai

I had been eating and cooking Pad Thai long before my Great Escape to Asia. This is one of Thailand's best-known dishes, consisting of noodles stir-fried with scrambled egg, beansprouts, shallots and, in this case, beef. Flat rice noodles are key for creating the right texture, and tamarind is essential to provide sourness.

In Thailand I learnt that this dish shouldn't be a greasy affair, but more delicate and drier. I saw endless variations of this dish, which included calamari, shrimp, chicken or tofu. You don't have to use just meat or fish, you can use all your favourites in one go.

Soak the rice noodles in warm water for about 10 minutes until flexible and pliable, but not overly soft, or cook according to the packet instructions (some dried noodles need to be blanched in boiling water for several minutes to soften them).

Meanwhile, combine the sugar, fish sauce, tamarind paste and chilli sauce in a small bowl and stir well. When ready, drain the noodles and set aside.

Heat the oil in a wok or a large non-stick frying pan until hot. Add the shallot, garlic and chilli and stir over a medium heat until fragrant. Tip in the beef and stir-fry for a minute so that the beef is still rare at this point. Remove the beef to a plate with a slotted spoon and set aside.

Drain the rice noodles and add to the wok with the sauce and a little splash of water. Stir-fry for a few minutes until they are tender. Push the ingredients in the wok to one side and add a little more oil to the other side. Crack the eggs over the oil and scramble lightly until they are almost cooked, and then fold into the noodles.

Return the beef to the wok and add the beansprouts and spring onions. Stir in the lime juice, palm sugar and soy sauces. Stir briefly over the heat, until the vegetables are slightly wilted but still crunchy.

Divide the pad Thai among warm, shallow serving bowls and sprinkle with the chopped peanuts. Serve immediately with the lime wedges.

Beef loc lac

Although it originated in Vietnam, this beef stir-fry was adopted and adapted by Khmer cuisine. *Loc lac* means 'shaking', which refers to the movement of the beef in the wok as it cooks. Cambodia has definitely marked this dish as its own, and in the major cities you won't have to travel far to find it on a menu.

There are many different preparations and variations of this recipe and I tried a fair few during my travels around Cambodia. The best version I ate was in Phnom Penh, in a lovely little corner-restaurant overlooking the river; the beef was perfectly seared and had just a slight tang of the marinade. So here is my recipe, inspired by that meal.

Place all the ingredients for the marinade in a bowl and mix together. Trim and cut the beef sirloin into thin strips, place in a bowl and cover with the marinade.

In a separate bowl, toss together the watercress, shallots and tomatoes and set aside. If you want to dress them, drizzle over some vegetable oil and rice vinegar.

Heat a wok or a large frying pan until hot then add a little groundnut oil, swirling the wok to coat the surface evenly. Remove the beef strips from the marinade and stir-fry for a couple of minutes with the garlic, ginger and chilli until the meat is nicely browned; for rare this is around 3–4 minutes. Around 30 seconds before serving, when the meat is cooked to your liking, add the remaining marinade to the wok, allow it to cook through and reduce slightly. Remove the beef from the wok and allow it to rest for a couple of minutes.

Meanwhile, prepare the tuk meric by combining all the ingredients, then divide this dipping sauce among individual dipping bowls. Place one bowl of dipping sauce on each plate with a quarter of the watercress salad. Lastly, divide the beef among the plates and serve immediately.

SERVES 4

BEEF
500g sirloin steak
1 bunch of watercress, washed
2 shallots, peeled and thinly sliced
12 cherry tomatoes, cut in half
vegetable oil and rice vinegar, for dressing (optional)
groundnut oil, for frying
4 garlic cloves, peeled and finely chopped
1 tbsp finely chopped ginger
1 red chilli, finely chopped

MARINADE
1 tbsp groundnut oil
3 tbsp dark sweet soy sauce
1 tbsp rice vinegar
2 tbsp palm sugar
1 tsp fish sauce

TUK MERIC
1 tsp Kampot peppercorns, lightly crushed
pinch of salt
juice of 2 limes

Nonya fried rice

SERVES 4

4 tbsp peanut or
  vegetable oil
3 eggs, lightly beaten
sea salt and freshly
  ground black pepper
3 garlic cloves, peeled
  and finely diced
5 shallots, peeled and
  finely sliced
1–2 red chillies, finely
  diced
15g dried prawns, finely
  ground
15g dried mushrooms
  (shiitake or black
  fungus), soaked
16 prawns, peeled and
  de-veined
½ small Chinese
  cabbage, shredded
1 tsp chilli paste
2 tbsp dark soy sauce
2 tbsp light soy sauce
300g cooked rice

GARNISH

2 spring onions, sliced
small handful of crispy
  shallots (see page 266)

This dish is a perfect example of how Malay kitchens recycle leftover rice. All over Southeast Asia, food waste is frowned upon, especially in the poorer regions where minimal or no wages mean that families have little to eat. To turn leftover rice into a nutritionally balanced meal, it is stir-fried with meat or fish, eggs and vegetables, and a delicious new dish can be created at little cost. Don't use freshly cooked rice for this, as the grains need to be firm so that they don't break down in the wok.

The distinctive taste of this dish comes from the Chinese ingredients of dried prawns, Chinese cabbage and mushrooms. You can eat it by itself, but it is usually served alongside fish crackers, a fried egg, Nonya fried chicken and salad.

Place a wok over a medium heat and add 2 tablespoons of oil. Swirl round the pan so that the surface is evenly coated. Pour in the beaten egg mixture and season. Fry the egg like an omelette, and turn it over so that it cooks on both sides. Remove from the pan, shred the omelette and set aside.

Clean the wok and add 2 tablespoons of oil. Toss in the garlic, shallots, chillies and dried prawns. Stir-fry for 1–2 minutes until fragrant and the ingredients are sizzling. Drain the mushrooms from the soaking water and thinly shred. Toss into the wok with the prawns, cabbage and chilli paste. Add a splash of water to loosen it, if necessary. Stir-fry for 1 minute until the prawns turn pink and the cabbage wilts slightly. Add the soy sauces and mix well. Lastly, toss in the rice and mix until evenly coated.

Divide among four plates or bowls and garnish with the spring onions and crispy shallots. Serve the shredded omelette on top.

Curries

Khmer chicken, aubergine, pumpkin and coconut curry

Kapitan chicken curry

Devil curry

Khmer monkfish and vegetable curry

Dry tomato, cauliflower and prawn curry

Massaman curry

Thai green chicken curry

Thai red curry with duck and lychees

Wesak Day vegetable curry

Khanom jeen

Yellow curry with cod and pineapple

Gaeng hung lay curry

Khmer chicken, aubergine, pumpkin and coconut curry

I first cooked this in Phnom Penh, Cambodia, at the training and education centre of Friends International, which is an amazing charitable organisation that provides a range of vocational training courses, including cooking, for street youths. The aim is to teach skills that will help them develop a career and improve their chances of employment. Since the charity began, in 1994, it has helped thousands of kids that otherwise would have had little or no help for a better future.

At the training centre I joined a group of 40 students, taught by chef Nina, who were studying the basic curriculum. Part of their training is to cook and serve lunch every day to the 1000 students and children in the centre. In the kitchen the students stood around tables prepping the food in their burgundy aprons and hats; some were slicing through orange pumpkin flesh, others were taking apart chicken and pounding spices to form aromatic pastes. When the prep was finished, the curry was cooked in large stockpots and the final result was truly delicious – one of the best curries I have had in a long time. This was true Cambodian cuisine, and after a week of eating tarantulas, duck egg foetus and crocodile (to name a few of the unusual foods), it was exciting to discover a Cambodian dish with mainstream ingredients. Friends International work hard to revive and rediscover Cambodian cuisine, which was severely affected during the Khmer Rouge reign.

So when it came to cooking a three-course meal for the people that I had met on my journey round Cambodia, I had to cook this dish. Using the recipe I learnt at the school as inspiration, I added a few extra ingredients and served it to my awaiting guests and royalty on a boat. I didn't have to worry about what the guests would think of it – they all loved it.

SERVES 4

400ml coconut milk
1 tbsp chilli paste
1 tsp shrimp paste
4–6 tbsp lemongrass paste (see page 267)
1 tbsp fish sauce
1 tbsp palm sugar, plus an extra pinch
1 tsp curry powder, plus an extra pinch
2 star anise
1 tsp ground cinnamon, plus an extra pinch
½ tsp ground coriander
2 kaffir lime leaves
1.5 litres chicken stock infused with galangal, garlic and chilli
450g chicken breast, cut into large dice
vegetable oil, for cooking
300g pumpkin, cut into large dice
pinch of chilli powder
pinch of salt
200g Thai baby aubergines, quartered

GARNISH

small handful of
  coriander leaves
1 Thai red chilli and
  1 Thai green chilli,
  finely sliced
zest of 1 lime

In a pan, reduce the coconut milk by half. Add the chilli, shrimp and lemongrass pastes and fish sauce and stir well. Add the palm sugar, curry powder, star anise, ground cinnamon and ground coriander and lime leaves and mix again. Cook gently for a few minutes to infuse.

In a separate saucepan, simmer the chicken stock infused with galangal, garlic and chilli. Place the chicken into the stock and poach for 8–10 minutes.

In a frying pan, heat 1 tablespoon of vegetable oil and sauté the pumpkin with a pinch each of ground cinnamon, curry powder, chilli powder, sugar and salt for a few minutes until golden. Remove and set aside. Heat another 2 tablespoons of oil in the pan and stir-fry the aubergine for a few minutes until golden.

Pour enough chicken stock over the curry paste to cover (about 200ml) then add the pumpkin and cook. Heat gently for a further 10–12 minutes, adding a touch more chicken stock to loosen, if necessary. Add the chicken pieces and aubergine and cook for a further 4–5 minutes to heat through.

Spoon into a serving bowl and garnish with coriander leaves, sliced chillies and lime zest. Serve.

SERVES 4

4 chicken thighs and
  4 legs, skin on and
  slashed
4 tbsp light soy sauce
4–6 tbsp dark sweet
  soy sauce
pinch of pepper
vegetable oil, for
  cooking
1 onion, peeled and
  finely chopped
400ml coconut milk
2–3 tbsp tamarind paste
4 kaffir lime leaves
1–2 tbsp palm sugar
small handful of
  coriander leaves,
  shredded, to serve

CURRY PASTE

6–8 dried red chillies,
  deseeded
2 lemongrass stalks,
  trimmed and sliced
2.5cm knob of turmeric
  root, peeled and
  chopped
5 shallots, peeled and
  chopped
2.5cm knob of ginger,
  peeled and chopped
2.5cm knob of galangal,
  peeled and chopped
4 candlenuts, or 1 tbsp
  macadamia nuts
1 tsp cinnamon powder
1 tbsp shrimp paste

Kapitan chicken curry

This recipe pays homage to a position created in the fifteenth century by the Portuguese – the Kapitan. These men were individuals of great standing who acted as administrators of the different ethnic communities. This curry is part of Nonya cuisine, bringing together Chinese and Malay influences. The base of the dish is a fragrant Malay curry paste with belacan (shrimp paste), to which is added chicken legs and thighs that have been marinated in a sweet, dark, Chinese soy sauce. The chicken is simmered with these flavourings and tamarind and coconut milk until the meat is tender and falling off the bone.

I first tried this in Penang, and I was impressed by its mouthwatering flavours, so when challenged to enter a *Nasi lemak* cooking competition (see page 214), I knew this had to be one of the dishes. Candlenuts are traditionally used in Malay cuisine to thicken sauces and need soaking first to soften them; the best substitute is the macadamia nut, as it is the closest in flavour and oil content.

Coat the chicken with the soy sauces and seasoning and mix well. Allow to marinate for up to an hour. To make the curry paste, blend all the ingredients together until smooth.

Heat a wok with 2 tablespoons of oil, then stir-fry the chicken with the marinade ingredients until it is partially cooked. Remove the chicken from the wok, reserving the oil. Set the chicken to one side. Add a touch more oil, if necessary, and sweat the onion in the pan, cooking for a few minutes to soften. Stir in the curry paste and fry for a further few minutes. Return the chicken and the marinating juices to the pan and add the coconut milk – the chicken should be nearly submerged in the liquid, if it isn't, top up with water. Reduce the heat, stir in the tamarind paste, lime leaves and palm sugar and allow to simmer for 45–50 minutes until the chicken is cooked through, adding a little water during cooking, if necessary.

To serve, remove the chicken from the bone (if desired) and arrange into serving dishes. Spoon the sauce on top and scatter with coriander leaves to serve.

Devil curry

This curry should come with flashing red lights and a big warning sign next to it, as it is incredibly spicy. It derives from the Eurasian cuisine formed by the intermarriage of Portuguese and Asians – Devil curry is one of its most famous offspring.

I always ask people I meet on my travels which recipes they would like to see in a book, and what their favourite or most interesting foods are. This curry was suggested by two wonderful ladies, Angela and Sharm, who work at the Berjaya culinary institute in Kuala Lumpur. They sold it to me by saying, 'It literally means taking a stick and shoving it into the gut and hurling it back out again. This curry can take you to hell and back.' If you are not prepared to ride this journey, I would suggest another curry, or you can add some yoghurt to calm down the spice!

Place all the ingredients for the curry paste in a pestle and mortar or blender and blend until smooth. Add some water to loosen the mixture, if needed.

Score the chicken skin then coat it in soy sauce and season. Place a wok or large saucepan over a medium heat and add 4 tablespoons of oil. Add the chicken and brown the skin, then remove it from the pan using a slotted spoon and set aside. Reserve the oil in the pan, toss in the onion, garlic, ginger and chillies and cook for 2–3 minutes until the onion is lightly golden. Remove from the pan and set aside.

Clean out the pan or wok and add 4 tablespoons of groundnut oil. Add the curry paste and cook until it browns and the oil turns red, as the chillies leak their colour. Dice the potatoes and add to the pan with the chicken and onion mixture and mix well. Add the white wine vinegar and reduce the liquid until almost evaporated. Add the mustard powder and cook for 1 minute, then add the chicken stock.

Reduce the heat, partially cover with a lid, and allow the curry to simmer for 40–45 minutes, until the chicken is tender and falling off the bone and the potatoes are soft. Season to taste.

Ladle the curry into warmed bowls and garnish with coriander. Serve alongside freshly cooked rice and some yoghurt.

SERVES 4

CURRY PASTE
2 lemongrass stalks, trimmed and chopped
4 garlic cloves, peeled and chopped
5 shallots, peeled and chopped
1cm knob of galangal, peeled
1cm knob of turmeric root, peeled
8–10 dried Kashmiri chillies, chopped
6–8 dried whole and 3 fresh red chillies, chopped
2 tbsp groundnut oil
2 candlenuts or 1 tsp macadamia nuts
½ tsp shrimp paste

CURRY
4 chicken thighs and 4 legs, skin on
1 tbsp dark sweet soy sauce
groundnut oil
1 onion, peeled and thinly sliced
3 garlic cloves, peeled and thinly sliced
2.5cm knob of ginger, peeled and thinly sliced
1–2 red chillies, halved
3 potatoes, peeled
100ml white wine vinegar
1 tbsp mustard powder
800ml chicken stock
handful of fresh coriander

Khmer monkfish and vegetable curry

Cambodian Khmer cuisine has been influenced by the fruits of its land for hundreds of years, and because fish is very widely available it is the most commonly cooked ingredient. While visiting a floating village called Prek Toal, along the Mekong delta, boats piled high with catfish chugged past at slow speed because of the sheer volume of fish caught. For these communities this is a way of life; for those with little or no money, the river provides them with the food they need to survive.

What I particularly liked about this curry was that there were no chillies in it (because in Cambodia they don't like their food spicy); it is an example of where rustic charm shines through and the simple flavours of the spices speak for themselves. My version uses monkfish; I love it and the meaty flakes hold well against the spices in this curry. If you don't like monkfish, substitute with any other firm white fish.

Mix together the curry powder, paprika, star anise and seasoning with 2 tablespoons of oil in a small bowl and set aside. Wash the monkfish in cold water and pat dry. Place in a bowl with the spice mixture, coat the monkfish all over and marinate for up to 30 minutes.

Place a medium-sized pan over a high heat, add some oil and carefully add the monkfish with the marinade and fry for a few minutes until cooked through. Carefully remove the monkfish and set aside.

Heat 2 tablespoons of oil in the pan, add the lemongrass paste and cook for 2–3 minutes until fragrant. Add the shallots, carrot, sweet potato and lime leaves. Cook for 3–4 minutes, coating them with the paste. Pour in the stock and simmer for 10 minutes until the carrot and potato are tender. Add all the remaining ingredients, including the monkfish, and simmer for 5 minutes, until all the ingredients are cooked through. Discard the star anise and lime leaves.

Divide the curry among four warmed bowls. Garnish with the coriander and lime wedges and serve with steamed jasmine rice (see page 267).

SERVES 4

2 tsp curry powder
2 tsp paprika
2 star anise
salt and freshly ground
  black pepper
vegetable oil, for frying
500g monkfish, cubed
2 tbsp lemongrass paste
  (see page 267)
2 shallots, peeled and
  thinly sliced
1 carrot, peeled and
  diced
1 sweet potato, peeled
  and diced
4 kaffir lime leaves
500ml fish stock
200g green beans, cut
  into 3cm pieces
1 tsp palm sugar (or soft
  brown sugar)
2 tbsp fish sauce

GARNISH

handful of coriander
  leaves, roughly torn
4 lime wedges

Dry tomato, cauliflower and prawn curry

SERVES 4–6

600g prawns, peeled
  and de-veined
1 tbsp turmeric powder,
  plus an extra dash
1 tbsp curry powder,
  plus an extra dash
pinch of salt
vegetable oil, for
  deep-frying
2 onions, peeled and
  finely diced
1 tbsp garlic paste
2 tbsp finely chopped
  ginger
1 tbsp fennel seeds
1 tbsp cumin seeds
1 tbsp coriander seeds
400ml coconut milk
1–2 tbsp tamarind paste
1 cinnamon stick
1–2 tsp palm sugar,
  to taste
1 medium cauliflower,
  cut into small florets
600g tomatoes,
  deseeded and diced
small handful of
  coriander leaves
1 red and 1 green chilli,
  finely sliced, to serve

Curries are often referred to as dry or wet; obviously a dry curry contains less liquid, while a wet curry takes on a more soup-like consistency. I am a fan of both, but this curry, with its Indian influence, lends itself to being dry. A local chef taught me that a common treatment of fish in Malaysia is to cook it with turmeric, allowing the fish to take on a golden yellow hue and a simple fragrant taste; the turmeric powder should be burnt in the oil and the fish deep-fried.

This was one of the three dishes I cooked in the *Nasi lemak* competition at the Berjaya culinary school in Kuala Lumpur, and because I needed to demonstrate the Indian influence in Malaysian cuisine, alongside the turmeric I added spices such as fennel seeds, coriander seeds, cumin seeds and curry powder. Serve this with a *Nasi lemak*.

Place the prawns in a bowl, add the turmeric, curry powder and salt and mix together well to coat. Heat a deep pan half-filled with oil and, once hot, deep-fry the prawns for 1–2 minutes until cooked. Remove from the oil and drain on kitchen paper.

Heat 2 tablespoons of oil in a frying pan and sauté the onions, garlic and ginger for a few minutes to soften. In a separate pan, toast the fennel, cumin and coriander seeds for 2 minutes. Once golden, transfer to a pestle and mortar and grind until fine, then add to the onion and garlic mixture and continue to cook for 2–3 minutes. Add the coconut milk and tamarind paste and mix well, then add the cinnamon stick and palm sugar.

Boil some water in a pan with a generous dash of turmeric, curry powder and seasoning. When boiling, add the cauliflower and cook for 3–4 minutes, until *al dente*. Drain the cauliflower and add to the curry sauce. Stir in the prawns, tomatoes and coriander leaves and mix well. Simmer for 4–5 minutes or until the coconut milk reduces and thickens so that there is enough liquid to coat the ingredients. Serve immediately, scattered with finely sliced red and green chillies.

SERVES 4

CURRY PASTE
1 tsp fennel seed
1 tsp cumin seeds
1 tsp coriander seeds
1 tsp cloves
vegetable oil, for frying
4 shallots, peeled and
  chopped
4 garlic cloves, peeled
  and chopped
2.5cm knob of galangal,
  peeled and chopped
2 lemongrass stalks,
  trimmed and chopped
3 kaffir lime leaves,
  roughly chopped
4 tbsp chilli paste
1 tsp shrimp paste
small handful of
  coriander stalks

CURRY
1kg stewing steak
salt and pepper
4 shallots, peeled and
  sliced
400ml coconut milk
1–1.2 litres beef stock
1 potato, peeled and
  diced
1 sweet potato, peeled
  and diced
1 tbsp fish sauce
1 tsp palm sugar
1 tbsp tamarind paste
2 bay leaves
1 cinnamon stick
4 tbsp roasted peanuts,
  to garnish
small handful of
  coriander leaves,
  to garnish

Massaman curry

Although Thailand is predominantly a Buddhist country, this dish derives from Southern Thailand and is of Muslim origin. In fact, the word Massaman is a linguistic variation of the Thai word for Muslim. This dish offers a twist on the typical Thai curry because it includes Indian spices such as cloves, fennel, coriander and cumin seeds. It reminds me of a winter stew; a hearty meal where little else is needed to fill you up.

If you have a slow cooker, this is the perfect dish for preparing in the morning for eating that evening, as the meat soaks up the spices and savoury-sweet flavours as it gently cooks. Or you can prepare it the day before and allow the aromas and flavours to deepen overnight. This is good made with lamb too.

Place a small frying pan over a medium heat and toast the fennel, cumin and coriander seeds and the cloves for 2 minutes, until golden brown and fragrant. Remove from the pan and set aside.

Place a wok over a medium heat and heat 2 tablespoons of oil. Lightly fry the shallots, garlic, galangal and lemongrass for 2–3 minutes until lightly browned. Place the toasted spices and fried flavourings into a blender or a mortar and pestle. Add the remaining curry paste ingredients and blend or mash until smooth.

Cut the stewing steak into 2cm chunks and season. Brown the meat in 2 tablespoons of oil in a wok – you may need to do this in batches. Remove the pan and set aside. Add the shallots and cook for 30 seconds until slightly caramelised. Add the curry paste and fry for 2 minutes or until golden brown. Pour in the coconut milk and mix well, allow it to reduce by a third then pour in the beef stock.

Return the beef to the pan with the potatoes, then add the fish sauce, palm sugar, tamarind, bay leaves, cinnamon stick and a pinch of salt. Lower the heat to a simmer, cover the pan and cook for 1½–2 hours, until the beef is tender, adding a touch of extra stock, if necessary.

When the curry is ready to serve, spoon it into a warmed bowl. Garnish with the roasted peanuts and coriander leaves and serve immediately.

Thai green chicken curry

Curries are a staple of Thai cuisine, but if there is one Thai dish that I have eaten more than any other, it's the Thai green curry – *Kaeng khiao wan*. The distinctive colour comes from the green paste, and the heat from the chillies used to make it. Pastes are a starting point for many Thai dishes, and a great curry paste can be prepared in minutes, but even if you buy a prepared paste it is important to remember that the strength and flavour will not be the same as that of a home-made one. In Thailand they like their food very spicy, but if you don't, adjust the amount of paste you use, because once it is in the curry you can't reduce the heat.

This moreish, sweet but spicy, fragranced, green-tinged sauce can play host to a variety of meat or vegetables, but here I have gone for a classic combination of chicken, exotic mushrooms (such as oyster, shiitake and enoki) and aubergine. This is best served with plain steamed rice.

Whiz all the ingredients for the curry paste together in a blender with 1–2 tablespoons of groundnut oil.

Heat a tablespoon of oil in a hot pan, add all of the curry paste and stir-fry for 2–3 minutes. Add the garlic, aubergine, mushrooms, carrot and peppercorns to the pan and stir-fry for 3 minutes. Skin and bone the chicken and cut into bite-sized pieces, add to the pan and cook for 2–3 minutes. Add the coconut milk, mix well and cook for 5 minutes. Add the chicken stock together with the palm sugar, lime leaves and fish sauce. Reduce the heat and simmer gently for 25–30 minutes.

Simmer until the aubergine and chicken are cooked, you may need to add a little water if the curry is too thick. Stir in the coriander and holy basil and cook for a further 1–2 minutes.

When the curry is ready, divide among four warmed bowls. Garnish with extra coriander and holy basil and serve immediately.

SERVES 4

CURRY PASTE
3–4 large green chillies, deseeded and chopped
4 garlic cloves, peeled and chopped
3 shallots, peeled and chopped
2 lemongrass stalks, trimmed and chopped
3 kaffir lime leaves
2 tsp ground coriander
1 tsp cumin seeds
2cm knob of galangal, peeled and chopped
2cm knob of ginger, peeled and chopped
handful of coriander stalks, chopped, plus 2 tbsp leaves
1 tsp salt

CURRY
groundnut oil
3 large garlic cloves, peeled and thinly sliced
1 large aubergine, roughly chopped
200g exotic mushrooms
1 medium carrot, peeled and diced
1 tsp fresh green peppercorns, drained
400g chicken thighs
400ml coconut milk
300ml chicken stock
1 tsp palm sugar
2 kaffir lime leaves
1 tbsp fish sauce
large handful coriander, roughly chopped, plus extra to garnish
2 tbsp holy basil, torn, plus extra to garnish

Thai red curry with duck and lychees

SERVES 4

CURRY PASTE

1 tsp cumin seeds

2 tbsp coriander seeds

1 tsp black peppercorns, crushed

10 dried Kashmiri chillies, soaked and drained

5 dried red chillies, soaked and drained

1 red long finger chilli, deseeded

2cm knob of galangal, peeled and chopped

3 kaffir limes leaves

5 garlic cloves, peeled and chopped

5 shallots, peeled and chopped

2 tbsp coriander stalks, chopped

1–2 lemongrass stalks, trimmed and chopped

1 tbsp shrimp paste

2 tsp sea salt

The Thai red curry is probably as well known as its counterpart, the Thai green curry. The all-important paste for this version is blended with aromatic spices such as cumin to give it its distinctive flavour, and it is the red chillies that provide the colour. Dried chillies work best in spice pastes as they leak their colouring better than fresh ones.

In Chiang Mai I was told that years ago in parts of Thailand, on certain occasions, all the men in the village would meet and spend a day making red curry paste – enough for a month. As I watched the wife of a household endlessly bashing ingredients with a mortar and pestle until finally, an hour later, the paste was formed, it occurred to me that this was a sensible idea. Although food processors mean you can make a paste in seconds, the result won't stay fresh for quite as long.

The combination of duck and lychees in this dish marries perfectly with the spicy coconut sauce. I ate a modern interpretation of this dish in Chiang Mai, which was served with rambutans – a close relation of the lychee. Here I have suggested serving one duck breast per person, to make it a more elegant dish.

Toast the cumin and coriander seeds in a dry pan, tossing them over a high heat for a few minutes until fragrant. Put the spices, with the remaining curry paste ingredients, into a blender or pestle and mortar and blend or pulse until smooth.

Next prepare the duck. Score the skin of the duck breasts in a criss-cross pattern with a very sharp knife. Season generously with salt and pepper and rub into the skin thoroughly. Place the duck breasts, skin-side down, in a dry, hot frying pan. Immediately turn down the heat and cook over a very low heat to render down the fat. This may take 8–10 minutes, depending on the thickness of the fat. Turn up the heat and fry until the skin is crisp. Turn the duck breasts over and cook the other side for another 3–4 minutes. Just before the duck is ready, drizzle over the honey and soy sauce. Toss and turn the

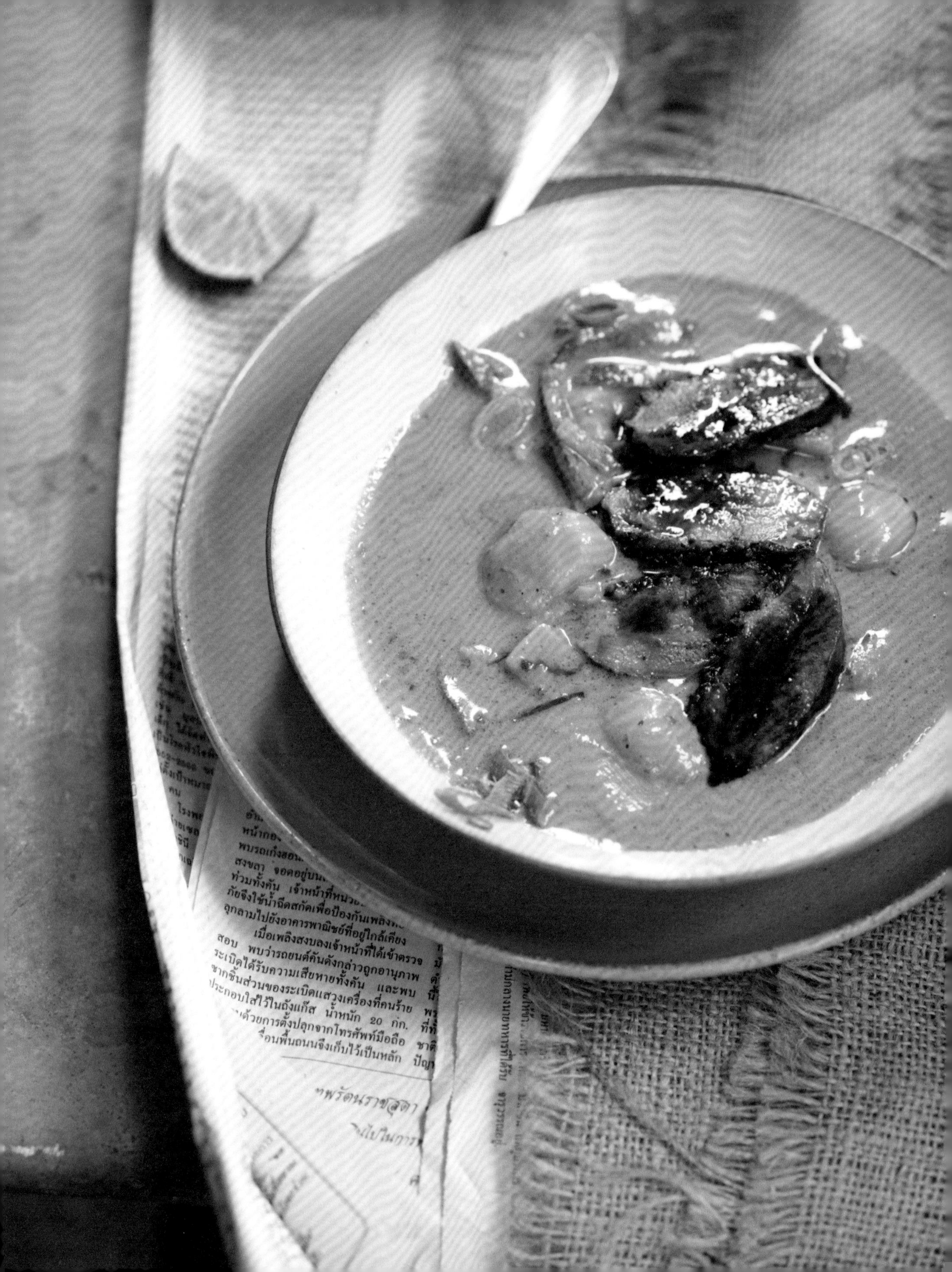

CURRY

4 x 175g duck breasts,
  skin on
sea salt and freshly
  ground black pepper
2 tbsp honey
2 tbsp dark soy sauce
groundnut oil, for
  cooking
400ml coconut milk
150ml chicken stock
1 tbsp fish sauce
1 tsp palm sugar
300g bamboo shoots,
  sliced lengthways
1 red pepper, thinly
  sliced
200g fresh lychees,
  peeled, stoned and
  quartered

GARNISH

handful of coriander
  leaves
2 limes, halved
2 spring onions, thinly
  sliced

duck in the honey and soy and cook until the liquid has reduced to a syrupy glaze. Transfer the duck to a warm plate and leave to rest for 5–10 minutes.

Place a wok or large saucepan over a high heat and add 3 tablespoons of groundnut oil. Add 4–6 tablespoons of the curry paste and fry for 1–2 minutes until the paste deepens in colour and smells fragrant. Pour in the coconut milk and chicken stock and stir well. Add the fish sauce and sugar and bring to a gentle simmer. Add in the remaining ingredients and allow the vegetables to cook through for 5 minutes.

Taste the curry and adjust the seasoning if necessary with more fish sauce or palm sugar. Slice the duck breasts and set aside.

Divide the curry among four warmed bowls and carefully place a sliced duck breast into each. Drizzle the glaze over the top. Garnish with the coriander, lime halves and spring onions. Serve with steamed jasmine rice (see page 267).

Wesak Day vegetable curry

As I travelled to the Buddhist Maha Vihara temple in Brickfields, Kuala Lumpur, at 9am on a national holiday, the traffic was almost at a standstill. Around 10,000 people were making their way there for Wesak Day, a celebration of Buddha's birthday and life. On arrival I was met by a woman called Sister Rupa, who had been cooking meals for the monks for 33 years, and at the age of 63 she was helping to run the kitchen for this huge event. Overnight, 10,000 meals were prepared by an army of volunteers to ensure that anyone who turned up to the temple would be fed.

Heat 3 tablespoons of oil in a large wok. Add the shallots along with a pinch of salt and sauté over a medium heat for a few minutes, to soften. Stir in the garlic and ginger and continue to heat for a further 1–2 minutes. Add the chillies, cinnamon stick, star anise, curry and chilli powders, mustard and fennel seeds to the pan and cook for a few minutes to release their flavours. Stir in the tomatoes and heat gently to soften.

Stir in the coconut milk with about 75ml water, bring to a simmer and cook gently for 10–15 minutes. Once reduced, stir in the tamarind paste to taste, followed by a pinch of sugar, curry leaves and lime zest. Continue to cook over a low heat while you prepare the vegetables.

Bring a saucepan half-filled with water to the boil. Add the turmeric, chillies, garlic, curry leaves, a pinch of salt, 2 tablespoons of sugar and the ginger and simmer for a few minutes to infuse. Cut the cauliflower into florets, peel the radish and chop it and cut the beans into small pieces. Add the vegetables to the pan and poach for 2–3 minutes until tender. Remove using a slotted spoon and add to the curry. Add the kerisik and stir to combine.

Cut the aubergine into small dice, and in a separate wok heat 2 tablespoons of oil and fry the aubergine with a pinch of salt for a few minutes, until golden. Drain through a colander into a bowl to remove any excess oil, then add to the curry. Check the seasoning, and amend accordingly, adding splash of water if necessary. Finally, stir in a squeeze of lime juice and chopped coriander before serving.

SERVES 4–6

- vegetable oil, for cooking
- 4 round shallots, peeled and diced
- sea salt
- 1 tbsp minced garlic
- 5cm knob of ginger, peeled and finely chopped
- 1 red and 1 green chilli, deseeded and finely chopped
- 1 cinnamon stick
- 1 star anise
- 1 tbsp medium curry powder
- ½ tsp mild chilli powder
- 1 tbsp mustard seeds
- 1 tsp fennel seeds
- 400g tomatoes, deseeded and diced
- 400ml coconut milk
- 1 tbsp tamarind paste
- sugar, to taste
- small handful of fresh curry leaves
- zest and juice of 1 lime
- small handful coriander leaves, chopped

VEGETABLES

- 1 tsp ground turmeric
- 1 Thai red and 1 Thai green chilli, cut in half
- 1 tbsp minced garlic
- 6–8 curry leaves
- 1 tbsp crushed ginger
- ½ cauliflower
- 1 small daikon radish
- 250–300g green beans
- 2 tbsp kerisik (see page 265)
- 1 large aubergine

SERVES 4

CURRY

300g cooked tuna or
  mackerel
4 tbsp Thai red curry
  paste (see page 162)
320ml coconut cream
250–300ml fish stock
5 kaffir lime leaves
1 tbsp palm sugar
1 tbsp fish sauce
400g thin rice noodles,
  blanched, to serve

GARNISH (OPTIONAL)

small handful of
  beansprouts, fresh
  or blanched
½ Chinese cabbage,
  core removed, leaves
  left whole
small handful of Thai
  basil leaves
small handful of
  mint leaves
small handful of
  coriander leaves
4 quails' eggs, boiled

Khanom jeen

My first encounter with this cross between a curry and a soup was near Krabi, in a tiny little village which consisted of a road lined with five houses and a stream next to the last house, a shared toilet and a plethora of plump chickens running around. A local lady, nicknamed 'Ya', had been invited to prepare some traditional Southern-Thai dishes for myself and the local family with whom I had spent the day. This was an opportunity to experience authentic regional Thai food.

I particularly liked this dish because the preparation was simple. Ya steamed some local tuna then flaked off the meat (a high-quality tinned tuna or mackerel in spring water is fine), mixed it together with some Thai red curry paste and simmered it in coconut cream. The finished curry was served over rice noodles and garnished with vegetables. Ya told me that this was one of her favourite dishes – and I completely understand why.

Place the fish in a mortar and pestle or blender, add the curry paste and mash or pulse together until the two are combined.

Place a medium-sized saucepan over a high heat and pour in half the coconut cream; bring it to the boil and allow it to reduce slightly. Stir in the curry paste and fish mixture. Allow this to simmer for 5 minutes, then taste for the strength of curry paste. If the mixture is not spicy enough, add another tablespoon of paste and mix well.

Add in the remaining coconut cream, fish stock, lime leaves, sugar and fish sauce, turn the heat down to low and allow the sauce to simmer for approximately 15 minutes.

Prepare the noodles according to the packet instructions and also prepare your preferred garnishes. Taste the sauce and adjust the seasoning as necessary, adding more palm sugar or fish sauce. To serve, divide the noodles between four plates, ladle the sauce over and top with your choice of garnish.

Yellow curry with cod and pineapple

When I eat out I often ask the kitchen to prepare a selection of dishes that they would recommend, rather than choose them myself. This doesn't always work in my favour, but when it does I'm always pleased to have taken the risk in order to discover something new. So, when this dish was placed in front of me at a hotel in Chiang Mai where the food was fusion-inspired and trendy, I knew it would taste as good as it looked.

The yellow curry is perhaps the least favoured of the Thai curries, but it is equally tasty. The distinctive yellow colour derives from the fresh turmeric, which is blended with red chillies and other aromatic ingredients. Yellow curry paste is spicy but lightly fragrant; to avoid the dish being overly sweet, tamarind is added to balance out the flavours and provide a necessary sour note. I have used cod in this curry, but any large white fish with a mild, slightly sweet-tasting flesh will work just as well.

Place all the ingredients for the curry paste in a pestle and mortar or blender and pulse or mash until smooth.

Wash and pat dry the cod fillets, then cut the fish into large chunks and set aside.

Heat 2 tablespoons of oil in a hot pan, add 4 tablespoons of the yellow curry paste and stir-fry for 2–3 minutes. Add the coconut milk, fish stock, tamarind paste and lime leaves and stir to combine. Bring the liquid to a simmer, then add the lime juice, palm sugar and fish sauce. Add the pineapple, mangetout and cherry tomatoes and cook for 5 minutes more. Add the cod pieces and poach them gently for 2–3 minutes until perfectly cooked.

When the curry is ready, divide it among four warmed bowls. Garnish with the coriander and lime halves. Serve immediately with some steamed rice.

SERVES 4

CURRY PASTE
5 red dried chillies, soaked, drained and roughly chopped
5cm knob of turmeric root, peeled and chopped
1–2 lemongrass stalks, trimmed and chopped
2cm knob of galangal, peeled and chopped
5 shallots, peeled and chopped
5 garlic cloves, peeled and chopped
2 tbsp shrimp paste
1 tsp salt
1 kaffir lime leaf

CURRY
4 x 175g skinless cod fillets
groundnut oil, for frying
200ml coconut milk
150–200ml fish stock
2–3 tbsp tamarind paste
2 kaffir lime leaves
juice of 1 lime
1 tbsp palm sugar
1 tbsp fish sauce
150g pineapple chunks
150g mangetout, trimmed
8 cherry tomatoes, halved

GARNISH
small handful of coriander leaves
2 limes, halved

Gaeng hung lay curry

Originally from Burma, this traditional Northern Thai dish consists of stewed pork belly and shoulder in a rich, dark, fragrant sauce finished with ginger and peanuts. It is typical of the food in the Chiang Mai region; it is lighter than in other areas as they use less coconut milk, and features meat because fresh fish is less readily available.

Gaeng hung lay is typically prepared at Buddhist blessings, so I served this curry alongside *Nam prik ong* (see page 204) to the monks who were conducting a house-blessing ceremony, during which affluence and good luck is bestowed upon the homeowner.

Like many Asian curries, the first step is to fry off the curry paste to release all the flavours, and then add the pork and curry powder. In Chiang Mai they make a specific curry powder for this recipe, although ordinary curry powder works just as well. What makes this curry different is the fresh ginger in it, which is less commonly cooked with in Thailand than its relative, galangal. The shredded ginger is sprinkled into the curry once it has cooked for 2 hours so that the tangy spicy notes remain prominent. Ideally this should be served with sticky rice, which is more commonly eaten in the north.

Grind together all the curry paste ingredients until smooth, either in a blender or pestle and mortar, with 2 tablespoons of water. Heat 4 tablespoons of oil in a large wok, add the paste and cook for a few minutes.

Place the pork belly and shoulder or leg in a large bowl and toss together with the curry powder and cinnamon to evenly coat. Add the pork to the pan with the curry paste and sauté for a few minutes. Add the fish sauce, oyster sauce, dark soy sauce and sugar and continue to cook for a few minutes to caramelise the pork.

Bash together the pickled garlic, if using, garlic and pickled ginger and add to the wok. Pour in the chicken stock and bring to the boil. Reduce the heat to a simmer, cover with foil or a lid and allow to cook gently for 1½–2 hours, until the meat is tender.

Towards the last 20 minutes of cooking, add the toasted peanuts and shredded ginger to the pan and continue to cook.

Spoon into bowls to serve and garnish with thinly sliced red chilli and more shredded ginger.

SERVES 4

CURRY PASTE
6–8 dried red chillies, rehydrated and roughly chopped
1 tsp salt
2 lemongrass stalks, trimmed and roughly sliced
2cm knob galangal, peeled and chopped
4 shallots, peeled and chopped
4 garlic cloves, peeled and chopped
1 tsp shrimp paste

PORK
vegetable oil, for cooking
500g pork belly, diced
500g pork shoulder or leg, diced
2 tsp curry powder
2 tsp ground cinnamon
4 tbsp fish sauce
4 tbsp oyster sauce
4 tbsp dark soy sauce
2 tbsp palm or cane sugar
1 tbsp pickled garlic (optional)
2 garlic cloves, peeled
2 tbsp pickled ginger, finely chopped
approx. 800ml chicken stock
100g toasted peanuts
2 tbsp shredded ginger

GARNISH
1 red chilli, finely sliced
2 tbsp shredded ginger

Fish

Fish amok

Prawn sambal

Pan-fried mackerel with a hot and sour sauce

Tamarind and orange halibut with a tomato and
pepper relish

Cambodian tamarind crab

Clay-pot caramelised cinnamon and ginger cod

Steamed sea bass with soy, lime and chilli

Stuffed squid with pork

Malay chilli fish parcels

MAKES APPROX. 12
250g lemon sole fillet,
  skin removed
12 small banana- leaf
  baskets (approx.
  5 x 5cm) or ramekins
  each lined with a
  kaffir lime leaf
coconut cream, to serve
4 kaffir lime leaves,
  shredded
1 red chilli, finely sliced
  on the diagonal

KROEUNG PASTE
2 tbsp lemongrass paste
  (see page 267)
2 garlic cloves, peeled
2 shallots, peeled and
  finely chopped
1 tbsp finely chopped
  galangal
1 tbsp finely chopped
  ginger
2 red long finger
  chillies, deseeded
½ tbsp ground turmeric
2 kaffir lime leaves,
  shredded
2 tbsp vegetable oil
200ml coconut cream
salt
1–2 tsp palm sugar
¼ tsp shrimp paste
1 tbsp fish sauce
1 egg, beaten

Fish amok

This unusual and unique fish recipe is regarded as one of the national dishes of Cambodia. It was Kethana Dunnet, owner of the Sugar Palm restaurant in Siem Reap, who introduced me to it. She explained that this *Amok trey* is believed to be an ancient royal recipe, supposedly originating in Angkor, however, like most written records in Cambodia, the documents were destroyed by the Khmer Rouge, so there is no evidence to support this claim.

This dish is surprisingly sophisticated, and when steamed it reminds me of a soufflé; each mouthful light and fragrant. In Cambodia they use local river fish, but I think lemon sole is a perfect replacement. While I was preparing this with Kethana, in the corner was a small army of workers skillfully preparing the baskets, but local Asian supermarkets will sell dried ones already made and these work very well. Alternatively, you can use a small soufflé dish or ramekin.

First make the kroeung. Put the lemongrass paste, garlic, shallots, galangal, ginger, chillies, turmeric and lime leaves in a food processor, add 1–2 tablespoons of oil and blend until smooth. Remove from the blender and tip into a bowl. Add the coconut cream, salt, palm sugar, shrimp paste, fish sauce and beaten egg and mix well.

To prepare the fish, cut the fillet into small pieces and add it to the kroeung. Allow to marinate for 10 minutes. Prepare a steamer, setting it over a pan on a medium heat.

Meanwhile, prepare the amoks by placing a lime leaf at the bottom of each ramekin if you are not using banana-leaf baskets. Spoon the amok mixture on top and repeat this process until all the ramekins are full and there is no mixture left. Place the ramekins or banana-leaf baskets in the steamer and cook for 8–10 minutes, or until the amok mixture has set and is cooked through. If they have not set, continue to steam for a further 2–3 minutes until ready.

When the amoks are set, spoon a little coconut cream on top and garnish with shredded lime leaves and chilli. Serve immediately.

Prawn sambal

SERVES 4

SPICE PASTE

15 dried Kashmiri
   chillies
4 whole dried chillies
4 shallots, peeled and
   chopped
½ tsp shrimp paste
2cm knob of ginger,
   peeled and chopped
2cm knob of turmeric,
   peeled and chopped

SAMBAL

vegetable oil, for
   cooking
1 onion, peeled and
   sliced
1 tbsp tamarind paste
1 tbsp coconut milk
   (optional)
1 tsp palm sugar
½ tsp salt
400g medium prawns,
   peeled and de-veined
150–200ml water

No *Nasi lemak* would be complete without a sambal – a chilli-based sauce. The most commonly cooked sambals in Malaysia include *ikan bilis*; tiny, dried, whole anchovies that are salty and crunchy at the same time. Mounds of these can be found piled up in the wet markets and they are delicious, but I find juicy prawns, *udang*, are an ideal replacement.

In Malaysia the dried chillies don't seem to pack as much of a punch as elsewhere, so when I cooked my sambal in the *Nasi lemak* competition I used 75 of them and, unbelievably, I was told that my sambal could have been hotter!

The redness in the sambal is provided by the dried red chillies; the more you use, the redder the colour. As Kashmiri ones are incredibly mild, using 15 will ensure that the sambal reaches the right hue. The dried long chillies provide the heat, so if you can take more heat, increase the amount you use.

Rehydrate the dried chillies in water for an hour or so, then squeeze out the liquid. Place them in the blender with all the other spice paste ingredients and blend to a fine paste. Add a little oil if it isn't smooth enough.

Place the onion in a pan with the oil and allow to caramelise for a few minutes over a low heat. Remove and set aside. Heat a dash more oil in the pan and fry the spice paste for 4–5 minutes or until the oil turns red and the mixture is cooked through. Continuously stir until the mixture turns a darker colour.

Return the onion to the pan, followed by the tamarind paste, coconut milk, if using, palm sugar and salt. Stir together. Add the prawns and cook for 1–2 minutes before adding the water. Simmer for 4–5 minutes to reduce the sauce, turn off the heat and serve immediately.

Pan-fried mackerel with a hot and sour sauce

Otherwise known as *Assam pedas* (*assam,* sour; *pedas,* spicy), this is a very popular dish in Malaysia. It is a perfect example of real home cooking and can be found bubbling away in kitchens all over Malaysia. Typically fish, fish heads or just vegetables are cooked in this, but the ingredients do vary.

I sampled this at a hawker stall, where they had fried whole mackerel first then finished it by cooking it in the sauce. As in all Malaysian cuisine, different cultures influence and contribute to recipes, and the version I tried had an Indian twist. I have always been an advocate of cooking mackerel, but I prefer it to be served as fillets – to avoid the small bones and make it easier to eat. I have refined this dish so that the fillets are pan-fried until crispy and the sauce is spooned over when plated, but it still retains its authenticity and flavour.

Place a small frying pan over a medium heat and toast the fennel, cumin, coriander and mustard seeds and cloves for 2 minutes until golden brown and fragrant. Grind the spices or bash in a mortar and pestle until fine. Remove from the pan and set aside. Add the curry powder and turmeric to the toasted ground spices and mix well.

Place a medium saucepan or large frying pan over a high heat and add 2 tablespoons of oil. Sweat the shallots, garlic and galangal and, after 2–3 minutes, add the ground spices, chilli and shrimp pastes. Fry until the spices coat the shallots and garlic and the pan is almost dry. Tip in the canned and fresh tomatoes, tamarind paste, palm sugar and 75–100ml water to loosen, then simmer for 15 minutes.

Score the mackerel skin with 3–4 incisions. Season with salt and pepper. Heat 2 tablespoons of oil in a frying pan and cook the mackerel, skin-side down, for 2–3 minutes until the skin is crispy. Turn over, cook for 30 seconds and remove from the heat. Transfer the fish to serving plates and spoon over the tomato sauce. Serve garnished with coriander leaves.

SERVES 4
8 mackerel fillets, pin-boned
small handful of fresh coriander leaves, to serve

SAUCE
1 tsp fennel seeds
1 tsp cumin seeds
1 tsp coriander seeds
1 tsp mustard seeds
½ tsp whole cloves
1 tsp curry powder
1 tsp ground turmeric
vegetable oil, for cooking
4 shallots, peeled and thinly sliced
2 garlic cloves, peeled and thinly diced
2cm knob of galangal, peeled and finely chopped
1 tbsp chilli paste
1 tsp shrimp paste
400g canned tomatoes
3 fresh tomatoes, diced
1 tbsp tamarind paste
1 tbsp palm sugar
salt and freshly ground black pepper

Tamarind and orange halibut with a tomato and pepper relish

This dish is inspired by my travels across Cambodia; not from one particular meal or dish, but from all over – the markets, the smells, the colours, the ingredients and the people. In a country where there are few cookbooks and nearly all literature and records were destroyed by the Khmer Rouge, this is my contribution to their cuisine.

The sweet meaty flesh of halibut is perfect with this fruity, sour marinade. If you can, leave the fish to marinate overnight so that the flesh can absorb all the flavours – it will also help it remain moist when cooked. The relish is a light accompaniment, adding a touch of freshness and a little texture to the dish.

Wash the halibut and pat dry with kitchen paper, then set aside. Place all the marinade ingredients in a pestle and mortar or food processor and blend or mash until almost smooth. Add a little oil to thin it, if needed. Rub each halibut fillet with the marinade, cover, then leave in the fridge to marinate for 1 hour, or preferably overnight.

To prepare the relish, heat 2 tablespoons of oil in a pan and sauté the shallots for a few minutes to soften. Stir in the pepper and tomatoes along with the vinegar, soy sauce and palm sugar. Reduce the heat and cook for 5–6 minutes until the tomatoes break down.

Place a large frying pan over a medium heat. Add 2 tablespoons of oil and fry the halibut, skin-side down, for 3–4 minutes. Flip over and cook the other side for 2–3 minutes, basting the halibut with more marinade as you cook the fish. The halibut is cooked to medium when the flesh is slightly springy to the touch.

When the fish is ready, remove it and set aside. Pour in the remaining marinade and cook until reduced and thickened. Pour over the fish and serve immediately, accompanied with the tomato relish and the basil scattered over.

SERVES 4

4 halibut fillets (each approx. 175–200g), skin on
vegetable oil, for cooking
large handful of holy basil, torn, to serve

MARINADE

4 tbsp tamarind paste
2 tsp finely chopped ginger
4 tbsp fish sauce
4 tbsp palm sugar
2 red chilli, deseeded and chopped
juice of 4 oranges
2 tsp salt
½ tsp finely chopped garlic

TOMATO RELISH

4 shallots, peeled and thinly sliced
1 yellow pepper, finely diced
300g cherry tomatoes, halved
2 tbsp rice vinegar
2 tbsp light soy sauce
1 tbsp palm sugar

**SERVES 4 AS A STARTER,
2 AS A MAIN**

2 large fresh cooked
  crabs, cleaned, cut
  into 4 parts and
  claws cracked
2 tbsp vegetable oil
6 shallots, peeled and
  thinly sliced
4 garlic cloves, peeled
  and thinly sliced
1 red long finger chilli,
  deseeded and sliced
1 green long finger
  chilli, deseeded
  and sliced
1 tbsp Kampot
  peppercorns, crushed
2 tbsp tamarind paste
1 tbsp rice wine
1 tbsp palm sugar
1 tbsp fish sauce
2 tbsp light soy sauce
4 spring onions,
  chopped, to garnish

Cambodian tamarind crab

As famous as Cambodia is for its Kampot pepper, it is equally well known for its crabs from the same region. South of Phnom Penh, the areas of Kep and Kampot serve up crabs daily, straight from the ocean, and from crab shacks to restaurants this local speciality is incredibly popular. This is not a dish for those who like to remain clean throughout their meal, though – it's all about rustic eating and delving in with your hands.

In Cambodia their local crabs are somewhat smaller than our larger native species; our Cromer crab is ideal for this recipe because the claws provide a generous amount of white meat.

If your crab is not already prepared, lay it on its back and twist off the front black-tipped claws – these contain most of the white meat. Put the crab with its eyes towards you and, using both hands, push up the six legs. Press both your thumbs on either side of the eyes and push away the 'purse' (the central body part). On the underside you will see a circle of grey feathery gills, called dead men's fingers. It is crucial you pull these off and discard them – they should not be eaten. Using a heavy knife, cut the round purse into four to expose the white meat. Pull the knuckles away from the claws and place the large claws on a worktop, then cover with a clean towel. Smash down with the back of a heavy knife or mallet until the shell cracks. Chop the body section in half. Alternatively, place a wooden board on top of the crab and hit it with a large hammer. Repeat with the other crab.

Place a wok over a medium heat and pour in the oil. When the oil is hot, toss in the shallots, garlic and chillies. Lightly fry for 30 seconds until the garlic is slightly browned.

Using a pestle and mortar, or the base of saucepan, lightly crush the Kampot peppercorns, then add them to the wok. Toss in the crab and stir-fry until some of the crab's juices have been released.

In a bowl, mix together the remaining ingredients and add to the wok. Stir-fry until the sauce has reduced slightly. Remove from the pan, garnish with the spring onions and serve immediately.

SERVES 4

4 x 200–250g skinned
  cod fillets
2 tsp ground cinnamon
salt and freshly ground
  black pepper
2 tbsp vegetable oil

SAUCE

4 garlic cloves, peeled
  and smashed
3–4 tbsp fish sauce
250ml water
4 star anise
2 cinnamon sticks
5cm knob of ginger,
  peeled and shredded
50g caster sugar

Clay-pot caramelised cinnamon and ginger cod

Often, the charm of a dish comes from the vessel in which it is cooked and served. Clay-pot cooking is popular all over Asia and further afield, but like every other country, Vietnam has developed its own recipes for this mighty pot, where they are called *Kho*. I first came across food cooked this way in a restaurant in Hanoi. Dainty clay pots with a delicately small serving of caramelised pork belly were flying out the kitchen, order after order. As the lid was lifted, the sweet smell of cinnamon filled the air. While I am a huge fan of pork belly, it struck me that a meaty fish such as cod would also work well with this combination of sweetness and spices.

This is often regarded as a great dish for those on a budget, as it needs only a handful of ingredients. However, I would recommend buying the freshest fish you can in order to get the best flavours. Cooking with a clay pot ensures that little moisture escapes while the fish is baking inside.

Preheat the oven to 180°C/Fan 160°C/Gas 4. To make the sauce, mix together the garlic, fish sauce, water, star anise, cinnamon sticks and shredded ginger in a bowl.

Pat dry the cod with kitchen paper and sprinkle over the ground cinnamon and a little seasoning. Place a frying pan over a medium heat and add the oil. Gently lay the fish away from you in the pan and sauté for 1–2 minutes on each side to colour the fish. Remove from the frying pan and place in a shallow baking dish or clay pot.

Meanwhile, in a separate pan, make a caramel for the sauce by dissolving the sugar over a medium heat. Once the sugar has nearly dissolved, add the mixed sauce ingredients and allow to simmer very gently until you reach a syrupy consistency.

Pour the sauce over the fish and bake in the oven for 10–12 minutes until cooked through. Remove from the oven and divide among warmed plates. Serve immediately, ideally alongside steamed rice.

Steamed sea bass with soy, lime and chilli

The delicate flavour of sea bass is ideal for this Thai preparation. One of my favourite ways to cook fish is 'en papillote', encasing the fish in a parcel so all the ingredients within it seep into the flesh and fragrance the fish.

This is an incredibly simple recipe, but if you aren't a fan of eating fish on the bone, ask your fishmonger to debone it, then cook the fillets as you would the whole fish, but halve the cooking time. The finished dish is visually stunning and can be served straight from the oven – which will impress a crowd.

Preheat the oven to 180°C/Fan 160°C/Gas 4. To prepare the sea bass, wash them in cold water and pat dry with kitchen paper. Carefully score the skins 3–4 times on each side using a sharp knife. Lightly season with salt and pepper.

Combine all the remaining ingredients, except the oil and the garnishes, in a bowl and mix together. Arrange a large sheet of foil, or baking parchment, on a flat surface and lightly grease with the oil. Drop a spoonful of the vegetable mixture in the centre and place a whole sea bass on top. Cover with another spoonful of mixture and enclose the foil or baking parchment to make a parcel. Repeat this with the remaining fish and mixture to make four parcels.

Place the parcels on a baking tray and cook for 25 minutes or until the fish is perfectly steamed through. Serve garnished with the chillies, spring onions, coriander and holy basil.

SERVES 4

4 small whole sea bass (each approx. 300g), scaled, gutted and fins removed
salt and pepper
6–8 tbsp light soy sauce
2 tsp fish sauce
6 shallots, peeled and thinly sliced
1 lemongrass stalk, trimmed and thinly sliced
juice and zest of 2 limes
2 carrots, peeled and julienned
4 garlic cloves, peeled and thinly sliced
5cm knob of ginger, peeled and shredded
vegetable oil, for greasing

GARNISH

2 Thai red chillies, finely sliced
4 spring onions, finely chopped
large handful of coriander, torn
large handful of holy basil, torn

Stuffed squid with pork

Every day in Mui Ne, either before dawn or after dusk, men and women paddle out into the ocean to go squid fishing in *thuyen thungs* – tiny round basket boats. Squid are lively and fast and not easy to catch, particularly from these small basket boats, but they are attracted to bright lights, so by fishing in darkness the fishermen's lights stand out and lure in the catch.

I joined Duc, a well-known Vietnamese chef-turned-translator, for a long and tiring stint squid fishing, after which he took me to a restaurant on the beachfront where he cooked his take on a Vietnamese squid dish. Traditionally, bean-thread noodles are also added into the stuffing, but for my recipe I have omitted these. After the mince is cooked and seasoned it is delicately stuffed inside the squid, which is then quickly fried until just a little browned. As the mince is already cooked, the squid only needs to be cooked for 30 seconds to 1 minute. It should be served with *Nuoc cham*, the classic Vietnamese dipping sauce.

First make the stuffing. Place a wok or frying pan over a medium heat and add 2 tablespoons of oil. Sweat the shallots, garlic and chilli for 2–3 minutes, to soften. Add the mushrooms and, when very hot, stir-fry them quickly until browned. Deglaze the pan with rice vinegar and let it reduce until nearly evaporated. Add the pork mince and pepper and fry. Using a wooden spoon, break down the mince. Add 4 tablespoons of water to the stuffing. Pour in the chicken stock with the fish sauce and palm sugar and simmer for 10 minutes. Stir in the chopped coriander for the last 1–2 minutes of cooking.

If your squid has tentacles, finely chop them and add to the stuffing. Simmer, then tip the stuffing into a bowl. Carefully stuff the mixture into each squid, using a toothpick to secure the ends. Repeat this process until all of the squid have been stuffed.

Heat 2 tablespoons of oil in a frying pan over a medium heat, add the squid and fry for 30 seconds–1 minute on each side for the baby squid, and 1–2 minutes on each side for the medium-sized squid. Carefully remove the squid from the pan and take out the toothpicks. Slice the squid into thirds or serve the baby squid whole, with the cooking juices poured over. Serve immediately with *nuoc cham*.

SERVES 4

8 medium squid or
 12 baby squid, cleaned
nuoc cham (see page
 266), to serve

STUFFING

vegetable oil, for frying
6 shallots, peeled and
 finely diced
2 garlic cloves, peeled
 and finely chopped
1 red chilli, finely
 chopped
50g oyster mushrooms,
 finely chopped
50g shiitake
 mushrooms, finely
 chopped
1–2 tbsp rice vinegar
250g pork mince
¼ tsp white pepper
150ml chicken stock
1 tbsp fish sauce
1 tsp palm sugar
small handful of
 chopped coriander
toothpicks, to secure

Malay chilli fish parcels

I cooked a fish dish very similar to this one on my Great Escape in India; the technique of wrapping fish in a banana leaf is a common cooking method throughout Asia and slightly further afield because it ensures that the flesh inside retains its moisture while cooking.

The difference between this and my Indian recipe is that the chilli paste is generously spread all over the fish before the banana leaf is delicately sealed with a toothpick. To help the paste ingredients mesh together, gently fry it off in a little oil prior to blending, to eliminate any rawness and acidity from the onions, garlic, ginger and galangal. You can spot these *Ikan bakar*, or 'burnt fish' parcels, on most hawker stalls, the give-away being the bright red paste that is exposed as the banana leaf is pulled away.

While I have opted to use snapper here, really any fish works well in this recipe – it is just about your personal preference. Of course, for meatier fish the cooking time should be extended. More than being just a decorative element or useful cooking tool, banana leaves also impart a light fragrance to the fish, but if you can't find banana leaves, use foil instead.

Preheat the oven to 220°C/Fan 200°C/Gas 7. Place all the paste ingredients except the oil in a blender and pulse until smooth. Heat the oil in a frying pan and fry the paste gently for 4–5 minutes. Allow to cool.

Wash the banana leaves in cold water, as they sometimes have a white chalky film on them. Pat dry with kitchen paper then carefully run the banana leaf over a naked flame to make it pliable.

Lightly score the snapper skin using a sharp knife and place the fish skin-side down onto the banana leaves. Spread the paste equally on top of each fillet. Wrap up the fish, folding in the edges of the banana leaves, and lay the packages in a shallow roasting tin so the joins are uppermost. Secure the parcels with toothpicks if the leaves won't stay flat. Leave to marinate for up to 1 hour, ideally.

Place the parcels in the oven and cook for 10–12 minutes, until the fish is cooked through.

Meanwhile, make the dipping sauce by mixing together all the ingredients until combined.

Remove the fish parcels from the oven and the baking dish. Carefully open up the banana leaves and serve immediately with the dipping sauce alongside and perhaps some simple stir-fried vegetables or fresh salad.

SERVES 4

4 large banana leaves
4 x red snapper (approx. 200g each), skin on, scaled and pin boned
toothpicks, to secure

PASTE

6 shallots, peeled and sliced
4 garlic cloves, peeled and sliced
2 lemongrass stalks, trimmed and sliced
2 tsp ground turmeric
1 tsp shrimp paste
2–4 dried chillies, soaked and roughly chopped
1 fresh red chilli
small handful of coriander stalks
2 tbsp water
4 tsp caster sugar
squeeze of lime juice
2cm knob of galangal, peeled and chopped
2 tbsp vegetable oil

DIPPING SAUCE

2 tbsp dark sweet soy sauce
juice of 2 limes
1 tbsp hot water
1 tsp palm sugar

Meat

Thai spicy beef-mince sauce

Vietnamese banh mi

Fragrant chicken leg

Roasted quail with fragrant pork stuffing

Char siew pork

Nasi lemak

Beef rendang

Beef short ribs braised in rice wine and spices

Nonya fried chicken

Vietnamese sweet and sour pork ribs

Vietnamese braised duck

Fire-roasted aubergine with spicy beef mince

Clay-pot chicken rice

Khmer wild honey-glazed roasted chicken

SERVES 4

CHILLI PASTE
4 shallots, peeled
  and sliced
2 garlic cloves, peeled
  and sliced
5 whole dried chillies,
  rehydrated and
  chopped
1 tsp shrimp paste
1 tsp soy bean paste

SAUCE
vegetable oil, for
  cooking
500g minced beef
1 tbsp oyster sauce
1 tbsp fish sauce
1 tbsp dark soy sauce
250g cherry tomatoes,
  halved
200ml beef stock

Thai spicy beef-mince sauce

This Northern Thai dish, known as *Nam prik ong*, is essentially a spicy meat dip which is served with fresh crunchy vegetables such as French beans, carrots, cabbage and cucumbers. It is traditionally made using fatty pork mince, but I have substituted this for beef mince, which I think offers a richer flavour.

Westerners often refer to this dish as the Thai version of spaghetti Bolognese, however the taste is incomparable. In this recipe the slowly cooked chillies and fresh tomatoes enrich the beef with a spicy sweetness, which comes from frying off the hot curry paste, thereby releasing the heat in the chillies. I was lucky enough to help cook this dish in Chiang Mai for a meal that was being prepared for local monks, friends and neighbours who had been invited to perform a house blessing. When I cooked it, the chilli paste was so strong that it nearly made my eyes water.

To prepare the chilli paste, place all the ingredients in a blender or mortar and pestle and pulse or grind until smooth.

Place a wok or large frying pan over a high heat and add 2 tablespoons of oil. Add the chilli paste and fry for 1 minute until aromatic. Add the minced beef and fry for 3–4 minutes, until the beef has browned and released its natural juices. Add the oyster sauce, fish sauce and soy sauce. Toss in the cherry tomatoes and beef stock and allow to simmer for 15 minutes, so that the tomatoes break down.

Simmer until ready and serve immediately alongside some noodles or, like they do in Thailand, with fresh vegetables.

Vietnamese banh mi

This Vietnamese 'sandwich' is so popular that I realised I had in fact eaten *Banh mi* in Europe long before my travels in Vietnam. Although the exact contents of this dish are open to personal interpretation, it should always consist of a baguette, pickled vegetables, meat (beef, pork or chicken – some *Banh mi* include all three!), fresh cucumber, coriander and a sauce such as chilli mayonnaise.

The Vietnamese often prepare pâtés as a sandwich filling, along with braised meats that cook for hours (the *Char siew* pork on page 210 or the Fragrant chicken leg on page 208 also make great fillings). For me, making a sandwich should be a quick affair, but I admit this recipe is not exactly simple. However, I have tried to compromise between the extended Vietnamese preparation and the simple English sandwich. I am, and will always remain, a fan of the humble steak sandwich, and so with a tender marinated rib-eye and some fresh cucumber and chilli mayonnaise, here is my *Banh mi.*

Place the steaks in a shallow dish. Mix the rest of the ingredients in a bowl and pour over the meat. Marinate for 3 hours or overnight.

Just before cooking, mix the carrot, daikon, salt, rice vinegar, sugar, chilli and garlic in a large bowl and toss together well. Prepare the cucumber. Combine the mayonnaise and chilli sauce and set aside.

Place a heavy-bottomed frying pan over a high heat, allow it to get smoking hot then add the steaks. Cook for 2½–3 minutes on each side for medium. If you like your steak well done, cook for another minute each side. If you like your steak rare, cook for a minute less on each side. Remove from the pan and rest for 5 minutes.

Slice the baguette lengthways. Slice each steak on the diagonal into 5 slices. Spread the chilli mayonnaise on both sides of the bread. Place the beef on the mayonnaise then pile on top the pickled vegetables, cucumber, red pepper and coriander, and sprinkle with sesame seeds. Top with the other half of bread. Slice the baguette into four and serve immediately.

SERVES 4

STEAK
2 x 300g rib-eye steaks
2 garlic cloves, peeled and finely chopped
2cm knob of ginger, peeled and finely chopped
1 lemongrass stalk, trimmed and finely sliced
3 tbsp vegetable oil
1 tbsp crushed black peppercorns
1 tbsp fish sauce
1 tsp dark soy sauce

PICKLED VEGETABLES
1 carrot, peeled and finely sliced
1 small daikon radish, peeled and finely sliced
pinch of salt
1–2 tbsp rice vinegar
2 tbsp sugar
½ chilli, deseeded and finely sliced
1 tsp finely chopped garlic

SANDWICH
½ cucumber, cut into long, wide strips using a vegetable peeler
4 tbsp mayonnaise
2 tbsp chilli sauce
crusty baguette
1 small red pepper, finely sliced
handful of fresh coriander leaves
1 tbsp sesame seeds

SERVES 4

4 chicken legs

1 garlic clove, peeled
  and chopped

3 shallots, peeled
  and diced

1 lemongrass stalk,
  trimmed and thinly
  sliced

3 kaffir lime leaves,
  thinly sliced

2cm knob of galangal,
  peeled and minced

1 tbsp coriander seeds

2 tbsp palm sugar

vegetable oil, for
  cooking

1 tsp salt

Fragrant chicken leg

This simple preparation of chicken leg, known as *Gai yang*, can be found on street stalls all over Thailand. Traditionally the legs are barbecued, and many of the stallholders demonstrated a clever technique to make turning the meat on the grill easier. they place the chicken legs in between chopsticks and fasten them together at the top with wire.

To make this more of an everyday recipe I have suggested grilling the legs first then finishing them off in the oven. However, if you are going to barbecue the legs, make sure you soak the chopsticks first to prevent them burning on the fire, then cook the chicken on the barbecue grill, turning it at intervals for 20–25 minutes, depending on the heat of the coals. The chicken is ready when the juices run clear.

I sampled *Gai yang* in Southern Thailand, where the vendor pulled the leg off the grill and wrapped it in a banana leaf, which was to be my plate. The stall next door sold *Som tam*, (Green papaya salad – see page 71), which completed my lunch. The two were a perfect combination, and one I would definitely recommend.

Preheat the oven 200°C/Fan 180°C/Gas 6. To prepare the chicken, pat dry the legs with kitchen paper and set aside. Score the skin a few times on each.

To prepare the marinade, place the remaining ingredients, except the oil and salt, in a mortar and pestle or blender and pulse or mash until smooth. If necessary, add a little oil. Sprinkle the chicken with salt then rub the marinade into the skin. Marinate for 1 hour or longer.

Heat a little oil in a griddle pan and, once hot, sear the chicken legs for 3–4 minutes on each side until chargrilled. Transfer to an ovenproof dish along with any marinade and bake in the oven.

Cook for 40–45 minutes, until the skin is crispy and the chicken tender and juicy. Serve immediately.

Roasted quail with fragrant pork stuffing

This recipe was inspired by a frog-hunting trip in a Cambodian village called Ra Loual, near Siem Reap, during which we were catching the frogs for Mrs Soto, who was going to stuff and cook them as part of a dinner she was preparing for guests. The river by her house was full of these jumping creatures, and with the help of a team of local boys we snared enough for dinner.

In Mrs Soto's outside kitchen she showed me her recipe: pork mince mixed together with kroeung – a Cambodian curry paste – which was delicately stuffed inside the frog. While Mrs Soto was fortunate enough to have a ready supply of frogs, for most of us that is not the case, but while cooking and chatting with her it occurred to me that quail would be a good substitute. I love quail; it is so delicate, cooks quickly and I thought it would work well with this unusual Asian twist. I have added an Asian vinaigrette here, to finish the dish and highlight its flavours.

Preheat the oven to 220°C/Fan 200°C/Gas 7. Rub the skin of the quails with salt and squeeze over the lime juice, then cover with cling film and chill for 30 minutes.

Meanwhile, prepare the stuffing. Place all the ingredients except the pork and peanuts in a food processor or pestle and mortar, adding a splash of water if necessary. Mash or blend until smooth and then mix into the ground pork. Add the peanuts. Heat 2 tablespoons of oil in a frying pan and fry off the paste for a few minutes. Allow to cool.

Remove the quails from the fridge and place on a baking tray. Stuff the quails with the kroeung mixture, dividing it equally among the birds. Drizzle the quail skins with oil, salt and pepper and cook for 20 minutes or until just cooked through (the juices should run clear when you pierce the thickest part of each quail with a skewer).

While the quails are cooking, make the dressing by simply whisking all the ingredients in a bowl until combined. Drizzle the dressing over the cooked quails and serve them alongside a fresh herb salad and steamed rice.

SERVES 4

4 oven-ready quails
salt and freshly ground
  black pepper
squeeze of lime juice
vegetable oil

STUFFING

2 lemongrass stalks,
  trimmed and roughly
  chopped
2 shallots, peeled and
  roughly chopped
2.5cm knob of galangal,
  peeled and chopped
1 tsp ground turmeric
4 kaffir lime leaves,
  shredded
3 garlic cloves, peeled
  and chopped
2 red chillies, deseeded
  and chopped
3 tsp fish sauce
pinch of ground white
  pepper
100–150g minced pork
2 tbsp roasted peanuts,
  roughly chopped

DRESSING

1 tbsp fish sauce
1 tbsp rice wine vinegar
juice of 1 lime
2 tbsp water
1 tbsp sugar
½ red chilli, deseeded
  and finely chopped
1 garlic clove, peeled
  and minced

SERVES 4–6

2 star anise
1 tsp salt
1 tsp peppercorns
1 tsp cinnamon
1 tsp Chinese five-spice
1kg pork belly
vegetable oil, for
  cooking

MARINADE

1 tbsp finely chopped
  garlic
1 tbsp finely chopped
  ginger
2 tbsp hoisin sauce
1 tbsp oyster sauce
1 tbsp honey
2 tbsp tomato ketchup
1 tbsp rice wine

GARNISH

1 small cucumber, cut
  into thin strips
handful of sesame
  seeds

Char siew pork

Despite its traditionally Chinese flavourings, this dish is very popular in Malaysia. It is instantly recognisable by the red charred coating on the pork, which is achieved by adding red food colouring – an ingredient I will not be using in my version.

Cooking pork belly until juicy and tender is a process that cannot be rushed. First the wrapped pork must be gently simmered, then unwrapped and slowly pan-fried to draw out the top layer of fat from the skin and allow it to crisp up. Once crisp, the pork belly is baked quickly in the oven to char the marinade. This three-step cooking method might seem a little cheffy and a lot of work, but it does ensure the pork stays beautifully moist beneath a crispy, charred exterior.

Grind the star anise, salt, peppercorns and cinnamon to a powder. Add the five-spice. Score the skin of the pork, rub over the spices, then very tightly wrap the meat in cling film, to lock in the flavours during poaching. Wrap a number of times, making sure there is no air trapped inside. Without breaking the cling film, change direction by 90 degrees and wrap the pork again. Push out any air and seal well. Place the pork in a large saucepan or stockpot big enough to fit the whole belly and cover with water. Simmer at the lowest heat with the lid on for 3 hours. Meanwhile, mix together the marinade for the pork and set aside until the pork belly is ready.

At the end of the cooking time, remove the pork from the water and carefully take off the cling film – don't worry if a little water has found its way in. Place the pork on a plate and cover with half the marinade, rubbing it into the meat and skin. Place the pork belly in a large non-stick frying pan, add a touch of oil and, over a low heat, cook for 25–30 minutes or until the skin is crispy.

Preheat the oven to 220°C/Fan 200°C/Gas 7. Transfer the pork to a wire rack set over a roasting tin and rub with the remaining marinade. Cook for 15–20 minutes until the marinade has charred round the edges, basting once during cooking. Remove from the oven, rest for 10–15 minutes then cut into slices and serve immediately with strips of cucumber and sesame seeds scattered over.

Nasi lemak

Once, this coconut rice was served only at breakfast, but this Malay staple is now eaten at any time of day and has become a national dish. While you can just eat it on its own, *Nasi lemak* is more commonly served alongside a hot spicy sambal sauce and a couple of meat or fish dishes. In Penang I was recommended a popular Nasi-lemak stall where I was offered a choice of 30–40 meat and fish accompaniments. However, no serving is complete without a garnish of fried peanuts, dried anchovies, cucumber and a boiled egg. For those eating on the go, everything is spooned into large newspaper sheets and tied up into a pyramidal cone shape.

As with any national dish, cooking a *Nasi lemak* is taken very seriously. Obtaining a delicate, fragrant, coconut flavour in the rice is imperative, and this derives from the pandan leaves that are added to the rice during cooking. Pandan leaves grow on fruit trees in Asia and have a light floral aroma. They can be purchased online or at Asian supermarkets and are well worth seeking out.

At the end of my epic journey round Malaysia I suddenly found myself entered into a *Nasi lemak* competition. It was going to be tough; my competitors were all women with extraordinary cooking talents who had had their whole lives to perfect this dish, whereas I, by comparison, had had just over a week to master it. Being quite a competitive person, I wanted to make sure my chances of winning were high, so at every opportunity I asked for tips and advice. While conducting my *Nasi lemak* survey, I was told by one chef that I should only cook with young coconut milk, another said to use coconut cream; a colleague recommended I soak the rice, another said I should wash the rice. All this advice just became confusing, so after speaking to nearly everyone I could on how to cook the perfect *Nasi lemak*, I came to the conclusion that I simply had to develop my own recipe and hope for the best.

For the competition I chose to serve my *Nasi lemak* with a prawn sambal, a Beef rendang (see page 218) and a chicken Kapitan (see page 150), and I was overwhelmed to be judged second out of six by an esteemed panel. When you prepare your *Nasi lemak*, choose your favourite accompanying dishes from any Malaysian curry, meat or fish dishes in this book, such as a combination of the Nonya fried chicken (see page 220), Pan-fried mackerel with a hot and sour sauce, or Devil curry (see page 151).

There is a lot of effort and organisation involved in this dish, so it's not one I would recommend if you just want a quick supper solution. However, the taste is well worth all the effort when you finally sit down to eat it!

Preheat the oven to 180°C/Fan 160°C/Gas 4. Arrange the anchovy fillets for the garnish on a non-stick baking tray, place in the oven and cook for 8–10 minutes until dry and firm. Remove and set aside.

Rinse the rice well in cold water until the water runs clear. Place it in a saucepan with the pandan leaves, if using, coconut milk, water, shallot, ginger, lemongrass and salt. Stir together, then bring to the boil and reduce the heat immediately. Cover with foil and simmer very gently for 8–10 minutes until all the liquid is absorbed and the rice is fluffy. Turn off the heat and leave to sit for 2–3 minutes.

For the soft-boiled eggs, place a small saucepan over a medium heat and bring to the boil. Gently lower in the eggs and cook for 6 minutes. Immediately remove them from the boiling water with a slotted spoon and place into ice-cold water to stop them cooking further.

To prepare the peanuts, deep-fry them in hot oil for 2 minutes until golden brown. Drain and remove, then set aside.

When the rice is ready, spoon onto a plate and garnish with the anchovies, soft-boiled eggs, cucumber and peanuts, then serve.

SERVES 4

300g basmati rice
2 pandan leaves, tied (optional)
100ml coconut milk
400ml water
1 shallot, peeled and sliced
2cm knob of ginger, peeled and sliced
1 lemongrass stalk, trimmed and bashed
generous pinch of salt

GARNISH

16 anchovy fillets in oil
4 eggs
60g peanuts
vegetable oil, for deep-frying
½ cucumber, diced

SERVES 4

PASTE

5cm knob of ginger,
  peeled and sliced
1 tsp ground turmeric
2.5cm knob of galangal,
  peeled
2 lemongrass stalks,
  white part only,
  chopped
1 fresh red long finger
  chilli
2 dried red chillies,
  rehydrated
6 shallots, peeled and
  chopped
4 garlic cloves, peeled
2 tsp fennel seeds
2 tsp cumin seeds
1 tsp ground coriander
1 star anise
5 cloves
1 tsp ground cinnamon

BEEF

4 tbsp vegetable oil
1kg stewing steak, diced
200ml coconut milk
4 kaffir lime leaves
2 tbsp tamarind paste
2 tbsp palm sugar
3 tbsp kerisik (optional,
  see page 265)

Beef rendang

As a dish that originated in Indonesia and was then adopted by Malaysia, Beef rendang can be described as a Malaysian–Asian beef stew, although some consider this a curry. I was taught to cook this in Malaysia by the best – a lady called Aunty Aini who came from the infamous matriarchal state of Negeri Sembilan. Her roadside café restaurant, aptly named 'Aunty Aini Café', showcases the most authentic Malay cuisine. The popularity of her food is to be seen every lunchtime, as there is rarely an empty seat in the place.

This dish is finished with kerisik, which is grated and toasted coconut that is pounded to a paste until the natural oils of the coconut leak out. Its brown colour is unusual, but it tastes delicious, adding an extra sweetness. While many Malaysians make kerisik by hand, many coconut stalls will sell it pre-made.

Make the rendang paste in batches. Place the ginger, turmeric, galangal and lemongrass in a blender. Add enough water to blend them to a smooth paste. Pulse, then transfer to a bowl and set aside. In the same blender, add the chillies, shallots, garlic and enough water to blend to a smooth paste. Pulse, then combine the pastes.

Place a small frying pan over a medium heat and toss in all the spices. Cook for 1–2 minutes until fragrant. Remove from the pan and grind to a powder. Toss the spices into the paste and mix well.

Heat 2–3 tablespoons of oil in a large wok or saucepan. Fry off the paste for a few minutes. Stir in the beef and sauté for 5–6 minutes. Add the coconut milk followed by 2 litres of water, the lime leaves, tamarind paste and palm sugar – you want the beef to be submerged.

Cook on a continuous low simmer for 2½–3 hours until the water has evaporated and the beef is tender. If at the end of the cooking time your beef is not tender, but the water has evaporated, top up with ½ litre water and cook until it has evaporated and the beef is tender. Eventually there should be a thick gravy at the bottom of the pan, just enough to coat the beef. When the beef is ready, remove from the heat and, if using, mix in the kerisik. Serve with *Nasi lemak*.

Beef short ribs braised in rice wine and spices

I love beef stews and this dish, *Bo oxt vang*, offers an exciting alternative. This recipe is a great example of the marriage of French and Vietnamese cuisines that has taken place in Vietnam. The traditional French cooking techniques shine through with the browning off of the meat and braising in rice wine (which in France would typically be red wine) with carrots, tomatoes, bay leaves and beef stock, which are complemented by Asian ingredients such as star anise, cinnamon, coriander seeds and dark sweet soy sauce.

Short ribs, also known as Jacob's ladder, is a beef cut taken from the top rib and has the bone in. These ribs require slow cooking, and as the meat becomes tender it breaks away from the bone and falls apart. You will probably need to order the beef from your butcher. A good alternative is stewing steak.

Preheat the oven to 160°C/Fan 140°C/Gas 3. Dust the ribs in seasoned flour. Heat a large casserole and add 2–3 tablespoons of oil. Season the beef and fry for 3–4 minutes until golden brown, then fry the other side until the meat is browned all over, adding more oil if necessary. Do this in batches, transferring the meat to a colander set over a bowl when browned.

Add the garlic, ginger, shallots, carrots, chillies, star anise, cinnamon sticks, coriander seeds and bay leaf to the casserole. Heat for 1–2 minutes then stir in the tomato purée. Cook for 2–3 minutes more. Deglaze the pan with the rice wine so the meat bobs up from the liquid but isn't completely covered. Bring to the boil and use a spoon to scrape the caramelised cooking juices from the bottom of the pan – this will give the stew more flavour. Return the beef to the pan. Top up with the stock, making sure the ribs are submerged in the liquid. Cover with a lid or foil and cook for 2 hours.

Remove the beef from the pan and set aside. Strain the liquid and return it to the casserole. Put the beef in the liquid with the tomatoes, soy sauce, fish sauce and honey. Return to the oven, covered, and cook for 1 hour. Serve immediately with steamed rice and vegetables.

SERVES 4

1.5kg short ribs, cut into individual ribs
sea salt and freshly ground black pepper
100g plain flour
4 tbsp vegetable oil
4 garlic cloves, peeled and diced
2cm knob of ginger, peeled and chopped
6 shallots, peeled and diced
2 carrots, peeled and diced
2 red long finger chillies, finely sliced
3 star anise
2 cinnamon sticks
1 tbsp coriander seeds
1 bay leaf
1 tbsp tomato purée
225ml rice wine
approx. 1–1.2 litres beef stock
400g fresh tomatoes, cored and diced
2 tbsp dark sweet soy sauce
2 tbsp fish sauce
2 tbsp honey

SERVES 4–6

16 pieces of chicken:
  wings, legs, thighs
approx. 1.3 litres milk
300g plain flour
2 tbsp sea salt
2 tbsp cracked black
  pepper
3 tbsp ground coriander
2 tbsp ground turmeric
1 tbsp cinnamon
2 tbsp ground cumin
2 tbsp garlic powder
2 tsp ground cloves
2 tbsp onion powder
1 tbsp cayenne pepper
vegetable oil, for frying

Nonya fried chicken

While it's not a dish for the weight-conscious, the crunchy coating that almost breaks off as you take the first mouthful, exposing the tender inner meat, can be dreamy when cooked to perfection. There is, however, great skill in achieving excellent fried chicken. I think the Malaysians have mastered the technique, just like the Americans, and I was surprised at how delicious fried chicken can be when full of spices.

I ate some of the best fried chicken in Kuala Lumpur as a snack in between filming, and it was that version, called *Inche kabin*, that inspired this recipe. Whether you have a deep-fat fryer or not, finish the cooking in the oven to ensure the coating is golden brown and the meat is fully cooked. This is a great dish for a crowd, but be prepared to have no leftovers.

In a large bowl, mix the chicken and 800ml of the milk and refrigerate overnight. Just before cooking, remove the chicken from the fridge and bring it to room temperature. Meanwhile, mix together all the dry ingredients, making sure the spices are well combined. Drizzle 2–3 tablespoons of the remaining fresh milk into the flour in small intervals, forking it through – you want the mixture a little lumpy. If you are using a deep-fat fryer, turn it on and set the temperature to 180°C. Alternatively, pour the oil into a large, deep saucepan, to a depth of about 7cm and place the pan over a medium heat.

Drain the chicken in a colander. Toss the chicken in the flour mixture to coat. Pour 400ml milk into a shallow bowl. Dip the chicken into the milk and then into the flour mixture again. Shake off any excess coating and set aside. Check the oil is up to temperature in the deep-fat fryer, or drop a piece of the breading into the oil in the pan – if it sizzles immediately you can start frying the chicken. Carefully add the chicken to the oil in batches, turning it to brown evenly. Preheat the oven to 180°C/Fan 160°C/Gas 4. Once the chicken is golden brown, remove from the oil and place on a wire rack to drain. Set on baking trays and cook in the oven for 30–35 minutes until all the flesh of the chicken is cooked. Remove and rest for 5–10 minutes before serving.

SAUCE

2 tbsp vegetable oil
2 onions, peeled and
  chopped
4–6 garlic cloves, peeled
  and chopped
2 tbsp finely chopped
  ginger
1 pineapple, peeled,
  cored and diced
2 tbsp chilli sauce
500g tomatoes, chopped
2 tbsp tamarind paste
1 tbsp rice vinegar
2–3 tbsp oyster sauce
1 tbsp fish sauce
palm sugar, to taste

RIBS

5cm knob of ginger,
  peeled and sliced
1 red long finger chilli,
  sliced lengthways and
  deseeded
1 lemongrass stalk,
  trimmed and bashed
800g pork ribs, cut into
  5cm pieces
6–8 spring onions,
  finely sliced, to
  garnish

Vietnamese sweet and sour pork ribs

I have always loved sweet and sour dishes, so I was excited to discover that this was a commonly cooked flavour combination in Vietnam. While I have eaten many different sweet and sour pork ribs, few have been of an Asian style, so when I was compiling my pork tasting menu for my last night in Hanoi, Vietnam, this had to be one of the seven dishes I prepared. I was pleased to hear that the restaurant where I was cooking has put this on their menu.

Tamarind is an amazing ingredient with a distinct sourness, and here it provides the sour element that is balanced out by the ripe sweetness of pineapple. It is important to caramelise the natural juices of the pineapple while cooking the sauce, as this enriches the dish. Personally I think the ribs should be eaten by hand, so you can chew every last bit of delicious meat off the bones. Sometimes eating should just be messy.

Place a large saucepan over a high heat, add the ginger, chilli and lemongrass, then the ribs, reduce the heat and cook for 20 minutes. Drain the ribs and pat dry with kitchen paper.

Meanwhile, prepare the sauce. Place a large pan over a medium heat and add the oil. Sauté the onions, garlic and ginger for 4–5 minutes. The onions should caramelise a little. Once soft, add the pineapple and caramelise for 4–5 minutes, the pineapple should soften and begin to release its natural juices. Add the chilli sauce, mix well, and cook for another 2 minutes. Toss in the tomatoes and cook for 5 minutes, so they break down. Mix the tamarind paste with 150ml water and add to the pan. Mix well. Add the rice vinegar, oyster sauce, fish sauce and sugar to taste. Allow to simmer for 10–15 minutes so that all the flavours incorporate.

Add the ribs to the sauce along with 100ml water. Cover and simmer for 30–45 minutes, until the ribs are tender and begin to fall away from the bone. Serve immediately, scattered with spring onions.

Vietnamese braised duck

While in Hanoi I spent an evening at a dedicated duck restaurant, at which, unusually, upon my arrival I was greeted by ducks waddling around. The Vietnamese are advocates of eating all their food as fresh as can be, especially meat, so this literally means slaughtering animals as close to eating as possible. I don't really need to say any more about my welcoming committee – their fate was already sealed.

Duck is not the most commonly eaten bird in Vietnam, but it is still popular and its gamey meat lends itself to Asian flavours. Duck should never be served dry, and this braising method is an excellent way to keep the flesh moist.

To prepare the sauce, place all the ingredients in a mixing bowl and set aside.

Score the duck's skin. Place a large casserole over a medium heat and add the duck pieces, skin-side down. Fry for 4–5 minutes until most of the fat has rendered down and the skin is golden brown. Turn the duck over and lightly brown the other side. Remove from the pan and keep warm. Remove three-quarters of the duck fat and set aside.

Place the onions, garlic, cinnamon stick, star anise and coriander seeds in the casserole and brown slightly in the duck fat – this should take 3–4 minutes. Add the sauce ingredients to the casserole and allow them to heat through, you want the sauce to start bubbling.

Return the duck to the casserole and mix well, so that it is totally covered with the sauce. Pour in the chicken stock and cover with the lid. Turn the heat down to its lowest setting and braise for 1½–1¾ hours. Check on the duck at this time, and if the meat isn't breaking away from the bone, leave it to carry on braising until ready.

When cooked, remove the duck from the casserole and set aside. Strain the sauce into a frying pan, discarding the onions and spices. Simmer down the remaining liquid for 20–30 minutes to a thick syrup. Drain off any excess fat and continue to cook, whisking if necessary. Pour the syrup over the duck and serve immediately.

SERVES 4

1 whole duck, jointed
sea salt and freshly
    ground black pepper
3 onions, peeled and
    roughly chopped
2 garlic cloves, peeled
    and chopped
1 cinnamon stick
2 star anise
1 tsp coriander seeds
2 litres chicken stock

SAUCE

1 tbsp each of finely
    chopped garlic
    and ginger
2 tbsp chilli paste
2 chillies, deseeded
    and finely sliced
1 tbsp lemongrass,
    finely sliced
2 tbsp oyster sauce
1 tbsp fish sauce
2 tbsp dark sweet
    soy sauce
2 tbsp coconut cream
1 tbsp honey
1 tbsp rice vinegar

❦

Fire-roasted aubergine with sweet beef mince

Cambodia's cuisine is amazingly varied and often surprising, and this recipe is no exception. Just like Fish amok, this dish appears frequently on local menus. While it may not look particularly appetising, one mouthful of the sweet mince with smoky notes of aubergine will sway your opinion.

I first saw this dish being served at the Sugar Palm restaurant in Siem Reap, where aubergines were being fire-roasted to order. The preparation is minimal, you just need to peel off some strips of skin around the aubergine then place it on a hob, or over coals, in direct contact with the flames. As the aubergine cooks it becomes soft to the touch and then bubbles of liquid start to gently ooze out of the skin. You can prepare the mince a day in advance, but the aubergines should always be cooked just prior to serving.

SERVES 4

4 medium aubergines

2 tbsp vegetable oil

6 shallots, peeled and
  thinly diced

4 garlic cloves, peeled
  and finely diced

2 lemongrass stalks,
  trimmed and
  thinly sliced

800g beef mince

4 tbsp oyster sauce

2 tbsp dark sweet
  soy sauce

3–4 tbsp fish sauce

2 tsp palm sugar

400ml beef stock

sea salt and freshly
  ground black pepper

small handful of
  coriander leaves

Using a vegetable peeler, peel away the skin from the top to the bottom of each aubergine in four strips at equal intervals. Place the aubergines directly onto an open flame or onto barbecue coals and cook for 10–15 minutes, turning frequently until charred all over. You want the aubergines to develop a smoky taste. If you don't have an open flame, cook them under a hot grill.

Meanwhile, prepare the beef. Place a medium-sized frying pan over a moderate heat and add the oil. Sweat the shallots, garlic and lemongrass for 2–3 minutes, to soften. Add the mince and fry so that it starts to release its own juices. While the beef mince is cooking, break it down so that it's fine, using a wooden spoon.

Once the beef is cooked, add the oyster, soy and fish sauces and palm sugar. Mix well then top up with the beef stock. Allow the beef to simmer for 10–15 minutes or until the stock has nearly evaporated. Taste for seasoning.

When the beef is ready, tear the aubergines apart to expose the soft flesh and spoon the mince on top. Garnish with coriander leaves and serve immediately.

Clay-pot chicken rice

This is the perfect one-pot wonder; only the bare minimum of effort is required to create this tasty Malaysian dish. In Penang I visited a food court where many of the stalls had simply six or seven clay pots cooking on the counter. One person manned the pots, and he would lift the lid and know just by sight if it was cooked and ready to serve.

This healthy, hearty meal includes myriad authentic ingredients, but many can be substituted for more-easily available ones without affecting the result. Jasmine rice is ideal in this because of its nutty aroma, and while I enjoy the chicken and rice combination, you can substitute other meats, or even fish, if they can be cooked quickly and lend themselves to steaming. *Lap cheong*, Chinese dried sausage, can be found in Asian or Chinese supermarkets or online, but if you can't find it, omit it. A clay pot is the optimum piece of kit, but an earthenware dish makes a good substitute or, as some Malay families do, you can cook the whole dish in a rice cooker.

Preheat the oven to 180°C/Fan 160°C/Gas 4. Combine all the marinade ingredients and pour over the chicken. Leave to marinate in the fridge for 1–3 hours. Rinse and briefly soak the rice in water – place the grains in a large bowl, half-fill it with cold running water and swish the rice with your fingers. Tip out the water, leaving the wet grains behind.

Heat the oil in a medium to large saucepan (or this can be done in a casserole if it is cast-iron) and sauté the shallots and garlic for a few minutes to soften. Add the marinated chicken, along with the marinade and cook until the chicken begins to brown. Add the mushrooms and Chinese sausage, if using, and stir together. Add the soaked rice, stir well and cook for a minute or two. Bring the stock to the boil in a pan and add to the rice and chicken. Transfer to a casserole, cover with foil and press it to the edges to seal, or use a lid.

Bake in the oven for 20–25 minutes until the rice is dry and the chicken is cooked through, adding a splash of extra stock if needed. Remove from the oven and serve garnished with sliced spring onions.

SERVES 4–6

- 4 chicken breasts or boneless chicken thighs, cut into bite-sized pieces
- 300g jasmine rice, uncooked
- 2 tbsp vegetable oil
- 4 shallots, peeled and thinly sliced
- 2 garlic cloves, peeled and diced
- 10–15g dried sliced shiitake mushrooms, rehydrated in water
- 3–4 Chinese sausages, thinly sliced (optional)
- approx. 800ml chicken stock

MARINADE

- 7.5cm knob of root ginger, peeled and grated
- 2 garlic cloves, peeled and finely chopped
- 1 tbsp light soy sauce
- 1 tbsp oyster sauce
- 1 tsp soft light brown sugar
- 1 tsp sesame oil
- ½ tsp ground white pepper
- ½ tsp cornflour
- 1 tsp sugar
- 1 tbsp rice vinegar
- 1 tbsp dark soy sauce
- 2 spring onions, sliced, to garnish

SERVES 4

1–1.2kg chicken
1 lemongrass stalk,
  finely chopped
2.5cm knob of galangal,
  finely chopped
1 red chilli, finely
  chopped
1 tbsp fish sauce
2 tbsp wild honey
1 tbsp rice wine
zest and juice of
  1 orange
1 tbsp dark soy sauce
4 tbsp vegetable oil
small handful of holy
  basil

Khmer wild honey-glazed roasted chicken

The two days I spent with the Mondulkiri tribe in Northern Cambodia provided me with great inspiration for a number of recipes, including this one. For this tribe, wild honey is an important part of the forest-based livelihoods upon which they depend. In the forest, bee-hunters climb impossibly high trees in order to harvest the precious honey, which is dark and rich in colour with a delicious earthy taste.

This dish is always prepared by the men in the village. The chicken is drizzled with a honey marinade then buried in a makeshift oven – a clay pot set in the ground and covered with charcoal. For simplicity, I have adapted this recipe to use an ordinary oven! To prevent the chicken's skin burning (because of the sugar in the honey), cover it for the first half of cooking, then uncover and continue to roast it so the skin can crisp up and colour and the marinade and natural juices can reduce to a dark sticky glaze. As Mondulkiri wild honey is only sold locally to the Mondulkiri tribe, I would suggest using the best-quality honey or wild honey you can get.

Preheat the oven to 220°C/Fan 200°C/Gas 7. Place the chicken in a large roasting tin. Mix together all the ingredients in a bowl, except the holy basil. Pour the marinade over the chicken, rub into the skin and scatter the holy basil leaves around it. Place the one of the squeezed orange halves in the cavity of the chicken. Cover tightly with tin foil, place in the oven and cook for 30 minutes.

After 30 minutes, remove the foil and baste the chicken with its juices and marinade. Reduce the heat to 180°C/Fan 160°C/Gas 4 and cook the chicken for another 30–40 minutes, until the juices of the chicken run clear when the thickest part of the thigh is pierced with a skewer. Remove from the oven and stir the liquid at the bottom of the tin to release any sticky areas. Allow the chicken to rest for 10 minutes.

Place the chicken on a serving platter and drain off all the liquid and juices, stirring them together. Pour over the chicken and serve.

Desserts/drinks

Watermelon and mango ice lollies

Melon salad with a lychee and mint sorbet

Vietnamese iced coffee

Sticky coconut rice with mango

Cinnamon and sweet potato pancakes

Chocolate-covered toasted sticky rice squares

Pineapple and mango crumble

Honey and jasmine pannacotta with a ginger papaya
  compote

Pineapple and coconut soufflé

Frozen chocolate and coconut pots

Lemongrass and kaffir lime crème brûlée

Pulled tea

Passion fruit jellies with lime cream

Strawberry and lime crush

Sticky rice, banana and peanut cakes

MAKES 6 ICE LOLLIES
450g watermelon, diced
180g mango, diced
50ml water
50g caster sugar
juice of ½ lime

Watermelon and mango ice lollies

While on my travels, the weather was often so hot that I just craved some juicy fresh fruit, and slices of cold watermelon were the perfect thirst quencher. Eaten on its own it is delicious, but I thought making ice lollies out of the bright-pink fruit would be fun and would make a refreshing dessert for all ages.

These little ice lollies are incredibly simple to prepare but have a mouthwatering taste. While watermelons are available without the seeds, if your fruit does have seeds do remove them before blending the flesh (unfortunately, this is a fiddly job). I would also recommend purchasing ice-lolly moulds; they are available to buy online or at any good kitchenware shop. A good alternative, though, is using small plastic cups and lolly sticks.

Pulse the watermelon and mango in a blender and set aside.

Place a small saucepan over a medium heat and add the water and sugar. Add the lime juice and drop in the squeezed lime half. Bring to the boil for 2–3 minutes, until a sugar syrup has formed. Allow to cool and remove the lime half.

Pour the sugar syrup into the blender and pulse with the fruit until smooth. Press the mixture through a sieve into a measuring jug to remove any remaining pips. Pour the strained mixture into ice-lolly moulds or small plastic cups. Place in the freezer for 1–1½ hours, until just about frozen. Place a stick or spoon in the centre of each lolly. Make sure that you leave the lollies in the freezer for a further hour, until completely frozen.

To serve, allow the lollies to stand at room temperature for 5 minutes before removing the mould or cup, or run them under warm water to release the lollies from their moulds.

Melon salad with a lychee and mint sorbet

The tropical climate of Southeast Asia is ideal for producing some of the most amazing fruits. A meal there is rarely complete without a plate of delicately carved melon, pineapple or papaya. In the very hot summer months, especially during my trip to Cambodia when they were experiencing a heatwave, a plate of fresh fruit was a welcome relief.

Everywhere on the stalls or at markets were piles of a little fruit called a rambutan. It is a relation of the lychee, and the visual resemblance can be seen in its small circular shape, bright-red skin and protruding soft hairs, but can also be experienced in its taste. While canned rambutans are available at specialist Asian stores, canned lychees (for the sorbet) are certainly more readily available. Either are suitable for this recipe. While admittedly it would be easier to just serve some lychees alongside perfectly ripe melon slices, the extra effort of making the sorbet does elevate a melon fruit salad to a dessert.

To make the sorbet, heat the lychee syrup in a pan with the lime juice and zest and reduce by half. Blend the lychees in a food processor and add to the syrup. Mix together to combine. Add the mint leaves to the mixture, and allow to infuse for 10–15 minutes or longer. Strain though a sieve and put in the fridge to chill. When cold, transfer to an ice-cream machine and churn for 20–25 minutes, or until frozen.

Meanwhile, halve the melons, remove and discard the seeds, then use a melon baller to carve out the flesh into balls (or simply cut it into small chunks, if you prefer). Divide the melon balls between individual serving bowls (or toss them together in a large salad bowl).

Finely grate the zest from the lime and orange over the fruit salad, then cut the citrus fruits in half and squeeze a little juice over each serving. Drizzle with the honey.

Spoon the sorbet on top and scatter over the shredded mint to serve.

SERVES 4

MELON SALAD
1 cantaloupe melon
1 honeydew or Gala melon
1 lime
1 orange
1–2 tsp runny honey
handful of mint, shredded, to serve

SORBET
3 tins of lychees (425g), plus 600ml lychee syrup
zest of 3 limes, juice of 2
small bunch of mint leaves

SERVES 4

strong dark roast coffee
 blend, preferably
 Vietnamese
4 tbsp condensed milk
ice (approx. 150g or as
 much as you prefer)

Vietnamese iced coffee

As one of the largest coffee producers in the world, the Vietnamese are proud of their coffee, and all over the country iced coffee is one of the most popular drinks. Traditionally the coffee is served in a small glass with ice and condensed milk at the bottom, and is brought to the tables, still brewing, in a Vietnamese coffee filter called a *phin*. When you are ready to drink, you open the filter and let the coffee drip out.

Although the consumption of dairy products in Southeast Asia (especially in countries such as Vietnam), remains minimal, condensed milk is popular because it doesn't need to be refrigerated. This coffee is so drinkable as to be almost addictive. Brew it to your desired strength, and if you find it too sweet, swap the condensed milk for cream.

Prepare the coffee in a French press or a Vietnamese coffee filter. Brew the coffee until it is at its strongest. Set aside to cool.

In the bottom of a glass, add 1 tablespoon of condensed milk. Top with a large amount of ice and pour the brewed coffee on top. With a tall spoon, mix together the condensed milk and coffee. Drink immediately.

Sticky coconut rice with mango

This *Khao niaow ma muang* is the Thai version of rice pudding. As rice is so important in the Thai diet, it is unsurprising that this is an incredibly popular dessert. Sticky rice is a short-grain rice that takes on a sticky consistency when cooked, hence the name. Unlike an English rice pudding, the sticky rice is cooked in water or just steamed.

This pudding is served with the coconut-flavoured sweet sauce poured over and with a few slices of fresh mango on the side. When choosing a ripe mango, check that the fruit smells fragrant and the flesh just gives way under the skin.

Soak the rice in water for 30 minutes, drain, then repeat this process. Place the rice in a saucepan and cover with the water. Add the lime juice and zest (reserving a touch of zest for garnish at the end), then place over a medium heat and bring to the boil. Reduce the heat to a bare simmer and allow the rice to steam through for 10 minutes or according to the packet instructions.

Meanwhile, place a small saucepan over a low heat and add the coconut milk, vanilla extract, sugar and salt. Do not allow the mixture to come to the boil, and stir until the sugar is dissolved, then remove from the heat. Pour this mixture into the steamed sticky rice along with the mango pieces, and fork through. Place a lid over the rice, allow the coconut milk to be absorbed into the grains, then set aside for 3–4 minutes.

Meanwhile, lightly toast the coconut in a dry frying pan over a medium heat until golden brown, shaking the pan frequently. Tip onto a plate and leave to cool.

Divide the rice pudding between serving bowls and scatter the desiccated coconut and toasted sesame seeds on top. Lightly scatter with any remaining lime zest and serve.

SERVES 4–6
200g Thai sticky rice
400ml water
juice and zest of 1 lime
400ml coconut milk
1 tsp vanilla extract
100g caster sugar
½ tsp salt
1 ripe mango, peeled and cut into small pieces
4 tbsp desiccated coconut
2 tbsp toasted sesame seeds

Cinnamon and sweet potato pancakes

MAKES 12

SWEET POTATO
1 sweet potato, peeled
  and diced
dash of vanilla essence
2 tsp caster sugar

PANCAKES
100g plain flour
1 tsp baking powder
½ tsp fine salt
4 tbsp caster sugar
2 tsp ground cinnamon
¼ tsp ground cloves
100ml milk
juice of ½ lime
1 large egg, beaten
2 tsp vanilla extract
2 large egg whites
butter, for frying

CARAMEL SAUCE
150g palm sugar
2 tbsp water
2 kaffir lime leaves,
  shredded
4 tbsp coconut cream

TO SERVE
vanilla ice cream

In Thailand, pancakes come in many shapes, sizes and flavours, such as coconut and sesame, pandan, taro, or plain stuffed with banana. Thai savoury food is often very sweet, but their desserts should be neither too sweet nor too savoury; in this recipe the boiled sweet potato is mildly sugary but it also adds an earthiness to the pancakes. Eaten alone these are very savoury, but the palm-sugar caramel counterbalances this.

Palm sugar is available in different forms, but in this recipe only the hard blocks will work. It varies in colour from batch to batch, but if you have a choice, buy the darker one. Lastly, only use fresh or frozen kaffir lime leaves here for the best scent.

Bring a small pan of water to the boil and add the potato, vanilla and sugar. Boil for 6–8 minutes until softened. Drain, letting the potato steam to remove excess moisture. Mash until smooth and set aside.

Sift the flour, baking powder, salt, sugar and spices into a large mixing bowl and make a well in the middle. Whisk together the milk and lime juice. Pour the egg, vanilla and a little of the milk mixture into the well and gradually incorporate the flour, whisking from the middle and working outwards until you have a thick, smooth paste. Add the rest of the milk mixture, a little at a time, whisking well between each addition, until you have a smooth batter. Whisk in the potato until smooth and beat until it is lump-free. Whisk the egg whites to medium-stiff peaks in a clean bowl, then fold into the batter.

Heat a teaspoon or two of butter in a large, heavy-based frying pan, then wipe the base with kitchen paper to grease it evenly. Pour in a ladleful of batter and fry for 1–2 minutes until golden underneath. Flip it over and cook for 45–60 seconds on the other side. Continue with the rest of the batter. Keep the pancakes warm in a low oven.

Gently heat the palm sugar and water in a pan to caramelise. Once dissolved, add the lime leaves and coconut cream and bubble together to form a rich caramel. Remove from the heat. Serve the pancakes on warmed plates with ice cream and the caramel poured over.

Chocolate-covered toasted sticky rice squares

One of my favourite food discoveries came in a place I least expected it to happen. While spending a couple of days in the jungle at a tribal wedding, I saw a member of the tribe toasting rice in a pan. This inspired me to create these little Cambodian petits fours set with honey, butter and sesame seeds. For a delicious finishing touch, the squares were half-dipped in melted dark chocolate and then crunchy desiccated coconut.

Even the Cambodian chefs that I cooked alongside for the final challenge had not seen anything like this before. The finished consistency is chewy and rich, the honey prominent. Keep them refrigerated until you serve them to preserve their texture.

Heat a large pan or wok and toast the sticky rice with the cinnamon sticks and star anise for 8–10 minutes, tossing frequently until golden brown. Remove the spices, transfer to a blender or pestle and mortar and blend or pound until the rice is fine.

Heat a frying pan over a medium heat, add the palm sugar, honey and butter and heat gently for a few minutes to dissolve the sugar and form a caramel. Stir in the ground rice and sesame seeds and mix well to combine. Remove from the heat.

Arrange a sheet of cling film on a flat surface and place the rice mixture on top – be careful, the mixture is very hot. Place another sheet of cling film on top and, using a rolling pin, roll until flattened and it has formed a large square. Transfer to a flat tray (still between the cling film) and chill for 2–3 hours. Once firm, remove from the fridge and remove the cling film. Cut into approximately 40 small squares or rectangles. Return to the fridge until needed.

Melt the dark chocolate in a bain marie. Remove from the heat, allow to cool slightly, then stir in the coconut cream. Dip the sticky rice pieces into the chocolate mixture then press into the desiccated coconut to coat. Return to the fridge until ready to serve.

MAKES APPROX. 40 PIECES

200g uncooked Thai sticky rice
2 cinnamon sticks
2 star anise
200g palm sugar
200g thick honey
30g unsalted butter
100g sesame seeds, toasted
100g dark chocolate
130ml coconut cream
100g desiccated coconut

SERVES 6

PANNACOTTA
600ml double cream
150ml coconut cream
50g caster sugar
a few drops of jasmine essence
1 vanilla pod, split in half and seeds scraped out
4 gelatine sheets
4 tbsp honey, plus 6 tsp for drizzling

COMPOTE
3 tbsp caster sugar
6 tbsp water
2 tbsp stem ginger, chopped
250g papaya, trimmed and chopped
150–200ml orange juice

Honey and jasmine pannacotta with a ginger papaya compote

This recipe is inspired by one of the best desserts that I ate during my whole Asian Great Escape – a honey, jasmine and coconut pannacotta prepared by a highly regarded Cambodian chef, Luu Meng, at his Phnom Penh restaurant, Malis. Luu Meng explained to me that edible flowers are commonly used in Cambodian cooking, which is evident at the fresh markets where the fruit and vegetable stalls are piled high with mounds of colourful petals. In this recipe the jasmine adds a light floral backdrop to the pannacotta. While jasmine essence is available, I would recommend using the fresh flowers if you can get them.

Put the cream, coconut cream, sugar, and jasmine essence in a large saucepan with the vanilla pod and seeds and allow the cream to infuse for 30 minutes. Place the pan over a low heat and stir, slowly bringing the liquid to a simmer. If it bubbles up the sides, lower the heat and simmer for 5 minutes until reduced by a third. Meanwhile, soak the gelatine in a bowl of cold water for a few minutes.

Remove the cream from the heat. Scoop out the gelatine sheets and gently squeeze out any excess water. Add the sheets to the cream and stir to dissolve. Allow to cool a little before stirring in the honey. Drizzle some honey in the base of six 150ml ramekins or dariole moulds, pass the pannacotta mixture through a sieve into a bowl then divide it evenly among the moulds. Chill for 2 hours until set.

Place the sugar and water in a saucepan and stir over a low heat to dissolve the sugar. Increase the heat and boil for 5 minutes until thickened slightly. Add the chopped ginger and allow to infuse for a minute or two. Add the papaya and orange juice, simmer for 5–6 minutes until the flesh becomes soft and pulpy. Transfer to a blender and blitz until smooth. Cool completely.

To serve, dip the base of each ramekin or mould briefly in hot water then invert them onto serving plates and shake to release. Serve with a spoonful of the ginger papaya compote on the side.

Pineapple and mango crumble

The humble crumble remains at the heart of English cuisine, but I believe it is a dessert that can be open to hundreds of different variations. The amazingly juicy mangoes of Cambodia and the beautiful yellow flesh of Thai pineapples inspired this Asian twist on a classic recipe. For many years I have adopted the technique of first making a caramel and then cooking the fruit in it; this ensures that the fruit part of the crumble is perfectly sweet and never dry.

If you are a big chilli fan, I would recommend adding a deseeded chopped red chilli into the fruit mixture before covering it with the topping, although I would pre-warn any guests that you are serving this to so they expect the unexpected! I have added macadamia nuts to the topping for some extra crunch, but these can be substituted with cashews, almonds or even peanuts.

Preheat the oven to 200°C/Fan 180°C/Gas 6. Gently heat the sugar in a pan until dissolved and beginning to caramelise. Once dissolved, add the pineapple and mango pieces with the fresh ginger, stem ginger and syrup, lime zest and juice. Toss to coat. Add the butter and shake the pan to combine. Allow the fruit to caramelise evenly, turning if necessary. Add a splash of dark rum and stand back as the alcohol may flambé. Cook for a further minute until the sauce is thick and syrupy.

Place all the crumble ingredients, except the macadamia nuts, in a food processor and blend until evenly combined (if you want to make your crumble mixture a little stickier, add a splash of water at this stage). Transfer the mixture to a bowl and stir in the chopped nuts.

Spoon the caramelised pineapple and mango into the bottom of an ovenproof baking dish (approximately 25 x 20 x 5cm). Sprinkle the crumble mixture on top and bake for 20–25 minutes until golden brown and bubbling.

Remove from the oven and serve with your favourite ice cream.

SERVES 6

100g caster sugar

1 pineapple, peeled, cored and diced

2 mangoes, peeled, cored and diced

5–7.5cm knob of ginger, peeled and finely grated

2cm knob of stem ginger, finely chopped, plus 4 tbsp syrup

zest and juice of 1 lime

40g unsalted butter, cut into cubes

splash of dark rum

CRUMBLE

175g plain flour

pinch of fine sea salt

100g cold unsalted butter, cut into cubes

75g demerara sugar

½ tsp ground cinnamon

50g ground rice powder (see page 266)

50g macadamia nuts, roughly chopped

Pineapple and coconut soufflé

The perfect soufflé can be an unforgettable dessert. While technically this dish requires some skill, I think a good result can be achieved through confidence. Admittedly this is not a dessert that you would find out on the streets of Cambodia or Vietnam, however, in Vietnam and Cambodia you will find French restaurants that serve up classic French dishes such as a soufflé – a remnant of the time when the French occupied both these countries.

To achieve the light, not too eggy, crispy on top and moist soufflé, fold the egg whites carefully into the pineapple base so they don't lose their air. My other trick is to apply a double layer of softened butter to the sides of the ramekins in upward strokes to help them rise evenly. Also, make sure the oven is up to temperature, before you put the ramekins in, otherwise they won't rise.

Peel and core the pineapple, then chop it into large pieces. Purée the pieces in a blender, with a touch of water, if necessary, until smooth. You may need to do this in batches. Place the purée in a sieve over a bowl and allow it to drain, pushing through with a spoon so you separate the pulp from the juice. (Save the juice for the syrup later.)

In a shallow, heavy-bottomed saucepan, stir the sugar and water over a medium heat for 2–3 minutes until the sugar caramelises. Add the pineapple purée and cook, stirring frequently for 4–5 minutes until the pineapple has cooked down and is light golden. (When you first stir in the purée the sugar will harden temporarily, but it will re-melt and incorporate with the pineapple as the fruit cooks down.) Tip into a small bowl to cool, then cover and refrigerate until needed.

In a medium, heavy-bottomed saucepan, bring the milk, vanilla pod and seeds to a fast simmer over a high heat. While the milk warms, combine the sugar, flour and butter in a medium bowl and rub together with your fingers to form a crumble.

Remove the vanilla pod from the milk and stir the liquid into the crumble. Cook, making sure you stir the sides and bottom to prevent burning, until the mix forms a paste and begins to ball up. Continue cooking until you see a thin, dry film on the bottom of the pan. Put the mixture in the bowl of a stand mixer (or in a large bowl if using a hand mixer) and, with the mixer running, whisk in the egg yolks, one at a time, until incorporated. Once combined, whisk in the pineapple reduction and continue to whisk until the soufflé base has cooled to room temperature. Set aside, or cover and refrigerate until needed.

Preheat the oven to 190°C/Fan 170°C/Gas 5. In a small bowl, combine the coconut with half the sugar. Lightly butter the sides of the ramekins, then dust with the coconut-sugar, shaking out any excess. In the bowl of a stand mixer (or in a large bowl if using a hand mixer), whisk the egg whites to soft peaks. Stir in the remaining sugar and whisk until you reach stiff glossy peaks. Place the soufflé base in a large bowl and fold in the egg whites gently. Spoon into the ramekins, using a palette knife to smooth the top and run your thumb around the inside edge of the ramekin. Place on a baking tray and bake for 15–18 minutes until well risen and light-golden brown.

Heat the pineapple juice and sugar in a pan for 8–10 minutes or until thickened and syrupy. Remove from the heat and set aside. Remove the soufflés from the oven. Dust with icing sugar, make a small incision in the centre of each and pour in some syrup. Serve immediately.

SERVES 4

1 large pineapple
2 tbsp sugar
1 tbsp water
icing sugar, sifted,
   to dust

SOUFFLÉ BASE

140ml milk
1 vanilla pod, split in
   half and seeds
   scraped out
1 tbsp caster sugar
30g plain flour
1 tbsp butter
2 egg yolks

SOUFFLÉ ASSEMBLY

2 tbsp desiccated
   coconut, toasted
   until golden
4 tbsp caster sugar
softened butter, for
   greasing the ramekins
3 egg whites

PINEAPPLE SYRUP

250ml pineapple juice
50g caster sugar

100ml condensed milk
200ml coconut cream
100ml double cream
2 tbsp cocoa powder,
   sifted, plus extra to
   decorate
100g dark chocolate
coconut shavings, to
   decorate

Frozen chocolate and coconut pots

While travelling round Hanoi, in Vietnam, I was asked what I would remember from that particular leg of the trip and, strangely enough, one of my answers was ice cream. In the unprecedentedly hot summer months, while walking along the street, standing next to their mopeds or even driving, people were eating ice-cream lollies.

I found out later that this trend was started over 50 years ago by a now famous ice-cream shop called *Kem trang tien*. To say that this shop was popular would be an understatement; it has to have its own security guard for crowd control and also for bike control (you can ride into the shop). Some days they can sell over 10,000 lollies and ice creams. It reminded me of a stock-market floor; hands and bodies pushing past each other to be served and as one counter sold out, the large crowd ran to the next counter, until there were none left. I have truly never seen such demand for ice cream. The flavours ranged from the traditional vanilla to the less traditional green bean, young rice and, the inspiration for this dessert, chocolate and coconut. This pudding requires little effort to achieve its decadent taste, but be warned that it is incredibly rich.

Place the condensed milk, coconut cream, double cream and cocoa powder in a bowl and whisk to mix it well.

Melt the chocolate in a bain marie or a bowl set over a pan of simmering water, and when fully melted pour into the cream mixture, whisking at the same time.

Divide the mixture among four ramekins and place in the freezer for 1–2 hours until set. Remove from the freezer around 5 minutes before serving, so that the pots soften, and serve with some coconut shavings scattered over and a dusting of cocoa powder.

Lemongrass and kaffir lime crème brûlée

SERVES 4

125ml whole milk

350ml double cream

1 vanilla pod, split

4–6 kaffir lime leaves

2 lemongrass stalks,
  trimmed and bashed

6 large egg yolks

75g caster sugar

4 tbsp demerara sugar

The custard base of a crème brûlée is perfect for infusing with many different flavours, in this case lemongrass and lime. These ingredients are more often used in savoury dishes, but the lemony fragrance from the lemongrass and the sweet citrus flavour from the kaffir lime gently add their Asian notes to this dessert without being overpowering.

The secret of a good crème brûlée is a really thin, crisp, caramel topping. The best way to achieve this is to put demerara sugar in a blender for a few seconds, creating a finer sugar that is then easier to sprinkle thinly on top. This ground sugar will caramelise quicker, though, so it is important to keep an eye on it and not burn or blacken the caramel, or it will taste bitter.

Pour the milk and cream into a saucepan. Scrape the seeds from the vanilla pod and add them to the pan, followed by the lime leaves and lemongrass. Bring the mixture to the boil, then remove from the heat and set aside to infuse for 1½–2 hours.

Preheat the oven to 150°C/Fan 130°C/Gas 2. Beat the egg yolks and caster sugar together until light and fluffy. Reheat the infused milk and cream and then strain it through a fine sieve. Pour into four ramekins, each about 125ml. Place the ramekins in a roasting tin half-filled with boiling water and bake for 50–55 minutes, or until set. Remove from the oven and allow to cool.

Dust the top of each brûlée with the demerara sugar. Using a blowtorch or under a very hot grill, caramelise the top, then serve immediately.

Pulled tea

SERVES 4
4 teabags
4 tbsp condensed milk
boiling water

This hot tea drink, *Teh tariq*, is served in a glass and can be found in almost any restaurant in Malaysia. It gets its name from the way in which it is prepared; a combination of black tea and condensed milk is pulled from one glass to another, which cools the liquids. The greater the height between the two glasses, the frothier the tea. If you prefer your tea to be less sweet, reduce the amount of condensed milk used. This is great fun to make!

Place the teabags in a teapot and fill with boiling water. Allow the tea to brew for a couple of minutes, or until the desired strength is reached.

When the tea is ready, divide it between four serving glasses. Add 1 tablespoon of condensed milk into each and mix well with a spoon. Take two separate large glasses and pour the tea from one of the serving glasses into one of these, then pass the tea between the two large glasses. As you do so, pull the glasses away from either other, as high as possible. Continue this process until the tea has become light and frothy, then return it to the serving glass. Serve immediately and repeat for the other servings.

Passion fruit jellies with lime cream

Jellies are popular across Asia as a dessert or sweet snack food, especially in Vietnam, Thailand and Cambodia. However, the jellies are not like those we are accustomed to, instead different setting agents such as agar agar and starches such as tapioca starch are used to create desserts with a jelly-like consistency. The ingredients differ too: in Thailand, savoury foods such as chestnuts, mung beans, sweetcorn and durian fruit are used in layered jelly desserts and drinks. As a compromise, here is my recipe for a more mainstream jelly with a tropical twist. Only fresh passion fruit will work here, as the passion fruit juices on the market tend to be sweetened.

Begin by making a sugar syrup. Dissolve the sugar in the water over a low heat, stirring frequently. Once the sugar has completely dissolved, increase the heat and bring to the boil. Slip in the lime zest and cook for 5 minutes. Remove from the heat and set aside.

Halve the passion fruits and squeeze their pulp and juice into a sieve set over a bowl. Rub the pulp and seeds with a wooden spoon to extract as much pulp and juice as possible (you are aiming for 150ml – top it up with orange juice if you run out of passion fruit). Reserve the seeds to use on top of the jellies.

Soak the gelatine leaves in cold water for a few minutes, then remove and squeeze out the excess water. Remove the lime zest from the sugar syrup then measure out 500ml into a clean pan. Reheat to almost boiling. Off the heat, stir in the passion-fruit juice then whisk in the gelatine until dissolved. Strain through a sieve into a jug and leave to cool. Divide the jelly among six small tumblers or moulds of approximately 100ml each, leaving a little room at the top. Chill for about 2 hours until set.

Whisk the cream with the icing sugar and lime zest and juice in a bowl, until you reach soft peaks. Chill until required.

To serve, spoon 1–2 tablespoons of the lime cream on top of each jelly. Decorate each with a teaspoon of the reserved passion-fruit seeds and touch of lime zest.

SERVES 6

PASSION FRUIT JELLY
200g caster sugar
500ml water
pared strips of zest from 1 lime, plus extra to decorate
12–14 ripe passion fruits
a little fresh orange juice (optional)
10 gelatine leaves

LIME CREAM
200ml double cream
3 tbsp icing sugar, sifted, to taste
zest of 1 lime, juice of ½

SERVES 4

800g fresh strawberries,
  hulled and quartered
50g caster sugar
500ml water
400g ice
juice of 1 lime
pinch of salt

Strawberry and lime crush

On my last day in Thailand I discovered an incredible drinks stall in a village called Bang Lung. The owners only had one blender and it worked overtime. The stall offered quite a few different drink combinations, but the strawberry looked the most appealing. Drinks in Thailand are often overly sweet, but the salt added at the end of this recipe really took the edge off the sugariness.

Place the chopped strawberries in a mixing bowl.

Place a medium saucepan over a high heat and add the sugar and water. Boil rapidly for 3–4 minutes until the liquid has slightly reduced and formed a syrup, then pour immediately over the strawberries. Cover with cling film and sit in the fridge for up to 3 hours to macerate, or overnight. You want the syrup to take on the same colour as the strawberries.

Make two drinks at a time. Put half the strawberries and half the ice in a blender. Squeeze in half the lime juice, add a sprinkle of salt and blend until frothy. Repeat this process again until you have all four drinks. Pour into tall glasses and drink immediately.

Sticky rice, banana and peanut cakes

While on long car journeys around Thailand, for a sweet snack I would nibble on *Khao tom mad* – little banana-leaf packages of coconut sticky rice and mashed sweet bananas. They were delicious. On occasion I had an amazing dessert that reminded me of sweet sushi – sticky rice rolled around bananas and set. So here I have combined the rich coconut flavours of the rice in the *Khao tom mad* with that sushi-roll element. This is a fun recipe that isn't too heavy. In Thailand they slice the rolled leaves before serving, but I think caramelising the banana and rice at the end makes this visually more appealing.

Place the rice in a pan with the coconut milk, water, vanilla pod, cinnamon sticks, star anise, nutmeg and brown sugar. Cook over a gentle heat for 12–14 minutes, stirring frequently, until the rice is cooked through and sticky. Lay out each banana leaf on a large sheet of cling film on a flat surface. You want 30cm squares, so cut the leaves if they are too big. Heat the butter and honey gently in a pan for a few minutes until thick and syrupy, then set aside.

Peel the bananas and lay two along one end of a banana leaf (so there's enough at either end of the bananad to tie later). Remove the bananas and scoop some cooled rice onto the leaf, patting it down to 1cm thick, as long as the bananas and twice as wide. Press the bananas back into the rice on each sheet (cut off the curved ends so they sit flat). Drizzle the honey mixture over the bananas and scatter with the peanuts. Roll the leaf so the rice completely surrounds the fruit, using the cling film to help. Tuck the edge of the leaf under and roll to the other side of the leaf – rolling as tightly as possible. Secure the ends of the roll with string. You should have enough rice left for one more roll. Place in the refrigerator and leave to set for at least 2 hours, or overnight. Or place in the freezer for 1–2 hours until set. Remove 5 minutes before serving to soften.

Remove the cling film and cut the rolls into 2.5cm pieces. Arrange on a serving plate. Dust with icing sugar and, using a blow-torch, glaze the cakes until golden and caramelised.

MAKES APPROX. 18 SLICES

200g Thai sticky rice
400ml coconut milk
150ml water
1 vanilla pod, split
  in half and seeds
  scraped out
2 cinnamon sticks
2 star anise
pinch of freshly grated
  nutmeg
40g light soft brown
  sugar
2 large banana leaves
30g butter
60g honey
4 medium bananas
70g roasted peanuts,
  crushed
icing sugar, sifted,
  to dust

Basics

CHICKEN STOCK
Makes about 1.5 litres

2 tbsp olive oil
1 large carrot, peeled and chopped
1 onion, peeled and chopped
2 celery sticks, trimmed and chopped
1 leek, trimmed and sliced
1 bay leaf
1 thyme sprig
3 garlic cloves, peeled
2 tbsp tomato purée
1kg raw chicken bones
about 2 litres water
sea salt and black pepper

Heat the oil in a stockpot. Add all the vegetables, herbs and garlic and sauté over a medium heat until the vegetables are golden. Stir in the tomato purée and cook for another minute.

Add the chicken bones and then pour in enough cold water to cover. Season lightly. Bring to the boil and skim off any scum that rises to the surface. Reduce the heat and leave to simmer gently for 1 hour.

Let the stock stand for a few minutes to cool slightly, before passing through a fine sieve into a bowl. Leave to cool. Either refrigerate and use within 5 days or freeze in portions for up to 3 months.

VEGETABLE STOCK (COURT BOUILLON)
Makes about 1.5 litres

1 leek, trimmed and chopped
1 carrot, peeled and chopped
½ celery stick, trimmed and chopped
1 onion, peeled and quartered
bouquet garni (few sprigs of thyme,
   tarragon and parsley, tied together)
¼ tsp white peppercorns
1 tsp rock salt
½ lemon, sliced
100ml dry white wine
1.5 litres water

Place all the ingredients in a medium saucepan and bring to the boil. Reduce the heat, cover and simmer for about 30 minutes. Strain the liquid through a fine sieve into a bowl or measuring jug, discarding all the vegetables and flavourings.

KERISIK
Makes 6 tbsp

100g fresh grated coconut

Heat a frying pan, and once hot add the grated coconut. Over a medium heat, toss frequently until golden brown. Remove from the pan, transfer to a pestle and mortar and grind until the coconut becomes a paste and the oil is released. This will take quite some time, about 10 minutes.

SAMBAL BELACAN
Makes 4 tbsp

6 dried red chillies
2 red long finger chillies, roughly chopped
1 tsp shrimp paste (belacan)
4 shallots, peeled and chopped
4 garlic cloves
squeeze of lime juice
1 tsp sugar

Soak the dried chillies in warm water. When softened, deseed and roughly chop. Grind or blend all the ingredients in a pestle and mortar or blender until smooth and place in the refrigerator until needed.

NUOC CHAM
Serves 8 as an accompaniment

2 tbsp granulated sugar
juice of 2 limes
2 red chillies, minced
3 garlic cloves, peeled and minced
5 tbsp water
1 tbsp rice vinegar
3 tbsp fish sauce
1 carrot, peeled and thinly shredded

In a small mixing bowl, dissolve the sugar in the lime juice. Add the remaining ingredients and stir to combine. Serve immediately or refrigerate, covered, for up to 3 days.

CRISPY SHALLOTS
Serves 6–8

6 shallots, peeled
3 tbsp plain flour
salt and pepper
vegetable oil, for frying

Thinly slice the shallots and separate out the slices. Dust the slices in enough flour to coat, shaking off any excess. In a wok or frying pan, pour a layer of vegetable oil to a depth of 2.5cm and set over a medium heat. Heat the oil until it immediately bubbles when you drop in one shallot slice. Fry the shallots for 45 seconds–1 minute or until golden brown and crispy. Remove immediately and drain. Allow the shallots to cool and season with salt and pepper. Serve immediately or store in an airtight container until needed.

GROUND RICE POWDER
Makes approx. 8 tbsp

100g sticky rice

In a heavy-bottomed frying pan or wok, toast the rice, stirring frequently for approximately 10–12 minutes or until golden brown. You want to brown the rice over a low heat so that the whole grain roasts. When the rice is ready, remove from the pan or wok and allow to cool completely before grinding to a fine powder in a food processor. Store in an airtight container until needed.

STEAMED JASMINE RICE
Serves 4

400g white jasmine rice
800ml water
pinch of salt
small knob of galangal, peeled and
    thinly sliced (optional)
1 lemongrass stalk, trimmed and
    bruised (optional)
zest of 1 lime (optional)

Rinse the rice under cold running water until it runs clear. Put the rice in a pan and add the water, along with a touch of salt. (If you want to add extra flavour, at this point add the galangal, lemongrass and lime zest.) Bring to the boil, then lower the heat and simmer for 10–15 minutes, covered, until all the water is absorbed. Alternatively, cook the rice in a rice cooker.

STICKY RICE
Serves 4

400g sticky rice
650ml water
pinch of salt

Soak the rice in a bowl of cold water for a few hours (or ideally overnight). Drain and rinse under cold running water. Place the rice in a large saucepan and cover with the water, adding the salt. Bring to a boil then reduce the heat to low, cover with a tight-fitting lid and simmer for 15 minutes or until the water is absorbed.

LEMONGRASS PASTE
Makes 4–6 tbsp

4 lemongrass stalks, white parts only, sliced
2.5cm knob of galangal, peeled and chopped
3cm knob of turmeric, peeled
1 kaffir lime leaf
2 garlic cloves, peeled
2 tbsp vegetable oil

Combine all the ingredients together in a blender and blend until smooth.

CHILLI PASTE
Makes approx. 5 tbsp

3 dried red chillies
6 fresh red chillies, roughly chopped
    (deseeded if you wish)
3 garlic cloves, peeled
1 tbsp vegetable oil
pinch of salt
touch of white wine vinegar

Soak the dried chillies in warm water until softened. Combine all the ingredients in a blender or processor and purée, adding enough water to form a thick paste.

Index

Acknowledgements

This book would not have been possible without the support of my incredibly talented and dedicated team. First I would like to thank Lauren Abery and Lisa Harrison for their extraordinary dedication and effort in working closely with me to put this book together, including helping to research and test the recipes and styling the food for photography. Chris Taylor for assisting on the shoot days and Dean for being chief taster and helping keep the kitchen in order during the testing phase of the recipes.

To the talented Emma Lee, thank you for the amazing photography, Emma Thomas for her superb prop styling and Patrick Budge for designing yet another vibrant and visually stunning book. My big thanks to the team at HarperCollins; Helena Caldon and Ione Walder for their fantastic editorial work and to everyone involved at the company in the production of the book from start to finish.

I am also so grateful to One Potato Two Potato for making this Great Escape possible. A huge thanks to all the team, including the incredibly talented Executive Producers Pat Llewellyn and Becky Clarke and Series Producer Amanda Murray and not forgetting the rest of the producing team: Emma, Christina, Tom, George, Tom, Naomi, Emma, Colin and Sarah DR. To Sean, Clare, Jeanette, Matt for making sure that we all got from A to B whilst travelling vast countries with seamless organisation. To the great crew that filmed me along the way: Danny, Russell and Stamos. Also thank you to the all the fixers for translating and speaking to the locals and chefs; without their help this book wouldn't have been possible.

I also have to say an endless thank you to Jennifer Aves-Elliot, my PA, who has one of the hardest jobs of balancing my diary and sorting out my life. To Chloe for doing what you do well so, the PR. Both jobs, a non-stop challenge and not for the faint-hearted.

Lastly, and most importantly, the biggest thank you in the world to my amazing wife Tana and our beautiful children – Megan, Jack, Holly and Tilly.